T H E   B O O K   O F

SALADS

T H E   B O O K   O F

SALADS

LORNA RHODES

Photographed by
SUE JORGENSEN

Published by Salamander Books Limited
LONDON • NEW YORK

Published 1989 by Salamander Books Ltd.,
52 Bedford Row, London WC1R 4LR

This book was created by Merehurst Limited
5 Great James Street, London WC1N 3DA

ISBN: 0 86101 392 1

Commissioned and directed by Merehurst Limited
Managing Editor: Felicity Jackson
Editor: Sarah Bush
Designer: Roger Daniels
Home Economist: Lorna Rhodes
Stylist: Carolyn Russell
Photographer: Sue Jorgensen, assisted by Des Adams
Typeset by Angel Graphics
Colour separation by Kentscan Limited
Printed in Belgium by Proost International Book Production

ACKNOWLEDGEMENTS

The publishers would like to thank the following
for their help:
The Glasshouse, 65 Long Acre, London WC2
Philips Home Appliances Group, 420-430 London Road,
Croydon CR9 3QR

Companion volumes of interest:
The Book of COCKTAILS
The Book of CHOCOLATES & PETITS FOURS
The Book of HORS D'OEUVRES
The Book of GARNISHES
The Book of PRESERVES
The Book of ICE CREAMS & SORBETS
The Book of GIFTS FROM THE PANTRY
The Book of PASTA
The Book of HOT & SPICY NIBBLES – DIPS – DISHES
The Book of CRÊPES & OMELETTES
The Book of FONDUES
The Book of BISCUITS
The Book of CHEESECAKES
The Book of PIZZAS & ITALIAN BREADS
The Book of GRILLING & BARBECUES
The Book of SOUPS
The Book of DRESSING & MARINADES
The Book of CHRISTMAS FOODS
The Book of SANDWICHES

CONTENTS

INTRODUCTION

A salad need never be the same each time it is made. The enormous variety of vegetables available all the year round can contribute to an ever-changing combination of colours, textures and flavours. Likewise, with international distribution so very much improved, supermarkets now stock the more exotic fruits and vegetables, and many of these recipes take advantage of this to create interesting dishes for family and friends, whatever the occasion.

Salads are the heart of healthy eating: they are rich source of many of the minerals, vitamins and other nutrients we need in our diet. To make a good salad you must always start with the freshest ingredients: crunchy vegetables, lean meats and poultry, low-calorie seafood, wholesome pasta, grains and beans. Whether prepared for a buffet, formal meal, family lunch or casual picnic, there are many simple salads using a variety of crisp leaves, raw and cooked vegetables, some with dressings, others without. There are recipes for starters, main courses and side dishes, including the new sophisticated *salades tièdes* that combine warm, freshly cooked ingredients, with cold ones for an added contrast. Some unusual partnerships have been created making use of fruits to add sweetness and colour or edible flowers such as nasturtiums, to give a special flourish.

There are more than 100 salad recipes in this book, all illustrated with beautiful colour photographs. Whatever the occasion and time of year, you will find a salad that uses seasonal produce.

SALAD LEAVES

Only the freshest of produce will do to make a good salad. Select leaves that are crisp, with a good colour. Try any of the following varieties, when available, mixing more than one in the salad bowl.

Round Lettuce, the most easily available lettuce, it looks like a soft cabbage with darker leaves on the outside becoming paler towards the centre.

Webb's Lettuce, with frilly outer leaves, it is crisp, sweet and juicy.

Cos Lettuce, also known as **Romaine,** has long feather-shaped, bright green leaves. It is used extensively throughout the Mediterranean.

Little Gem Lettuce, a miniature cos, only 10 cm (4 in) long, is paler in colour.

Iceberg Lettuce, is very pale green. The crisp leaves are tightly packed.

Batavia, also known as **Escarole,** is a variety of endive but with broader only slightly curled leaves. It has a slightly bitter taste that stands up to a stronger flavoured dressing.

Endive, also known as **Frisée,** is large and very frilly with dark green outer leaves and pale yellow leaves in the centre. Crisp in texture and slightly bitter in flavour, it is often mixed with other leaves.

Lamb's Lettuce, also known as **Corn Salad** or **Maché,** is easily recognisable because of its dark green, tongue-shaped leaves which grow in clusters.

Radicchio, a member of the chicory family, looks like a large purple Brussels sprout. The wonderful coloured leaves brighten up salads.

Lollo Rosso, with very frizzy red edged leaves, makes a pretty addition to the salad bowl.

Oakleaf Lettuce, also known as **Red Salad Bowl,** has floppy leaves that resemble oak leaves in shape. They are purplish red on the outside going to green in the centre.

Chicory, a spear-shaped vegetable with tightly packed white leaves which can be separated or chopped.

Chinese Leaves, also known as

Chinese Cabbage, is shaped like a cos lettuce and has crinkly, pale green and white leaves.

Spinach is a useful leaf, especially for warm salads and to provide contrast with sharper flavours.

DRESSINGS

A well-made dressing will enhance the flavours of the salad ingredients and add the final touch. Dressings tend to fall into two main categories, the oil and vinegar ones known as vinaigrette, and egg and oil dressings known as mayonnaise. In addition, there are low-calorie dressings based on yogurt, and citrus juices.

The type of oil used makes a great difference to the flavour of the vinaigrette or mayonnaise. In many cases, extra virgin olive oil, which is a cold pressed oil, is recommended, but it does have a strong, distinctive flavour that can overwhelm delicate ingredients. Sun-

flower, safflower or grapeseed oils have less pronounced flavours and make good alternatives, either on their own or mixed with the olive oil.

Nut oils such as walnut and hazelnut add extra flavour to salads, as do light and dark sesame oils – the darker having the stronger flavour. These unusual oils can be rather overpowering when used alone and are often mixed with sunflower oil to make a dressing.

Buy two or three good quality vinegars for your dressings. Choose from cider, wine and sherry vinegars, or ones which are flavoured with fruit, herbs or spices. Do not use malt vinegar as the flavour is too strong for salads. Lemon juice can be used instead of vinegar.

Choose fine, aromatic French mustard, sea salt and freshly ground pepper to season; add an unusual touch by grinding a mixture of different coloured peppercorns over the top of a salad.

VINAIGRETTE DRESSING

½ teaspoon salt
pepper
½ teaspoon Dijon mustard
½ teaspoon sugar
6 teaspoons wine vinegar
90 ml (3 fl oz/⅓ cup) olive oil

Put salt, pepper, mustard, sugar and vinegar into a bowl and stir together until salt and sugar have dissolved.

Pour in oil and whisk with a fork to combine well.

Alternatively, place ingredients in a screw-top jar and shake well until blended.

Makes about 125 ml (4 fl oz/½ cup).

Note: Use less oil if a sharper dressing is preferred. Use cider or herb-flavoured vinegar, or substitute lemon juice for the wine vinegar.

VARIATIONS

For Garlic Vinaigrette: Add 1 or 2 crushed cloves of garlic to the dressing.

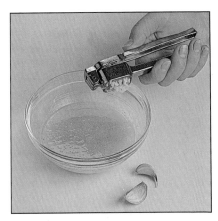

For Herb Vinaigrette: Add 1-2 tablespoons of chopped fresh herbs, such as parsley, chervil, basil, tarragon or chives, or a mixture.

For Honey Vinaigrette: Substitute 1 teaspoon clear honey for the sugar in the dressing.

For Light Vinaigrette: Replace half or all of the olive oil with sunflower oil.

MAYONNAISE

1 egg yolk
pinch salt
½ teaspoon Dijon mustard
155 ml (5 fl oz/⅔ cup) olive oil
2 teaspoons wine vinegar or lemon juice

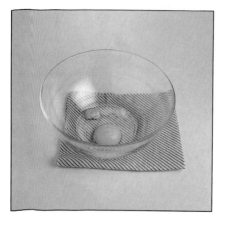

Have all the ingredients at room temperature: this will help prevent curdling. Put egg yolk, salt and mustard into a bowl. Stand bowl on a damp cloth to stop it sliding about.

Whisk ingredients together, then begin to add oil, drop by drop, whisking all the time.

As mayonnaise thickens, add oil in a steady trickle. When all oil has been added, beat in vinegar or lemon juice. The mayonnaise can be thinned by the addition of a little hot water, if necessary.

Makes 155 ml (5 fl oz/⅔ cup).

——— VARIATIONS ———

For Quicker Blender Mayonnaise:
Using the same ingredients, put the egg yolk, salt and mustard into a blender. Work for 15 seconds, then add oil slowly, quickening as the mayonnaise thickens. Work in the vinegar, then season, if necessary.

For Herb Mayonnaise: Add 2 tablespoons chopped fresh herbs, such as parsley, chives or tarragon, or a mixture.

For Garlic Mayonnaise (Aïoli):
Add 2 crushed cloves of garlic to the egg yolk before adding the oil.

For Light Mayonnaise: Replace either half or all the olive oil with sunflower oil, and whisk in 2 tablespoons natural yogurt.

YOGURT DRESSING

| 155 ml (5 fl oz/⅔ cup) natural yogurt |
| 2 tablespoons lemon juice |
| 1 teaspoon Dijon mustard |
| 1 teaspoon clear honey |
| salt and pepper |

Put all the ingredients into a bowl and whisk together until the honey is blended in. Cover the bowl and refrigerate before using.

Makes 155 ml (5 fl oz/⅔ cup).

Variations: Add 2 tablespoons chopped fresh herbs such as tarragon, mint, parsley, chives, or a mixture.

Alternatively, add 1 crushed clove of garlic to the dressing.

Note: This dressing is a low-calorie alternative to mayonnaise.

ORIENTAL DRESSING

| 90 ml (3 fl oz/⅓ cup) sunflower oil |
| 4 teaspoons dark soy sauce |
| 3 teaspoons dry sherry |
| 1 clove garlic, crushed |
| 1 teaspoon clear honey |
| ½ teaspoon five-spice powder |

Mix ingredients together in a bowl or screw-top jar.

Makes about 155 ml (5 fl oz/⅔ cup).

For Sesame Dressing: Mix together 2 tablespoons sunflower oil, 2 teaspoons dark sesame oil, 1 tablespoon light soy sauce, 1 teaspoon clear honey and 2 teaspoons rice vinegar.

For Chinese Dressing: Mix together 2 tablespoons sunflower oil, 1 tablespoon light sesame oil, 1 tablespoon chilli vinegar and 1 tablespoon light soy sauce.

COMPOSED SALAD

4 tiny artichokes
125 g (4 oz) thin green beans, trimmed if desired
1 lettuce
1 head fennel
½ bunch radishes
2 carrots, finely grated
½ quantity Garlic Vinaigrette, see page 11
1 quantity Garlic Mayonnaise, see page 13
fennel fronds, to garnish

Trim artichoke stalks, then cook in a saucepan of simmering water for 25-30 minutes, until tender. Drain and cool. Cook beans for 3 minutes. Drain and cool.

To assemble salad, arrange a few lettuce leaves, to one side, on 4 plates. Slice fennel and arrange attractively with beans, radishes and carrot.

Remove a few outer artichoke leaves and arrange on plates. Cut artichokes in half, remove the hairy chokes. Place 2 halves on each plate. Spoon a little garlic dressing into each half. Garnish with fennel fronds.

Serve salads with garlic mayonnaise.

Serves 4.

Variation: Use a selection of ingredients, such as hard-boiled quails' eggs, cooked baby sweetcorn, celery pieces, cooked broad beans or grated jicame. (Jicame is a turnip-shaped vegetable which resembles the water chestnut in taste and texture. It is now widely available from larger supermarkets.)

CEVICHE

500 g (1 lb) fish fillets, such as plaice, flounder, cod, lemon sole, mackerel or bass

juice of 5 limes

2 tablespoons olive oil

2 cloves garlic, finely chopped

3 tomatoes, skinned, seeded and chopped

1 green chilli, seeded and finely chopped

1 onion, finely chopped

12 green olives, stoned

2 tablespoons chopped fresh coriander

salt and pepper

½ avocado

lime slices and coriander leaves, to garnish

Skin fish, cut into thin slices or small chunks. Place in a glass dish and pour over lime juice. Cover and refrigerate for 24 hours.

Next day, heat oil, cook garlic until coloured slightly. Remove from heat, leave to cool, then add tomatoes, chilli, onion, olives and coriander. Season with salt and pepper.

Drain fish, add to sauce, making sure all the fish is well coated, then cover bowl and chill.

To serve, divide fish and sauce between 4 dishes. Peel and slice avocado. Place a few slices on each plate.

Garnish with lime slices and coriander leaves.

Serves 4.

—— SEAFOOD IN WINE JELLY ——

185 g (6 oz) salmon steak, cut in half
12 queen scallops or 6 medium scallops
375 ml (12 fl oz/1½ cups) dry white wine
salt and white pepper
250 ml (8 fl oz/1 cup) fish stock, strained
3 teaspoons powdered gelatine
185 g (6 oz) peeled cooked prawns
dill sprigs
SAFFRON DRESSING:
3 teaspoons olive oil
1 shallot, chopped
pinch saffron threads
3 tablespoons double (thick) cream

Put salmon and scallops into a pan with 155 ml (5 fl oz/⅔ cup) of the wine. Season with salt and pepper, then simmer for 5-6 minutes. Allow fish to cool in cooking liquid.

Pour half the stock into bowl. Sprinkle gelatine over and leave to soften for 2-3 minutes. Stand bowl in a saucepan of hot water; stir until dissolved. Add remaining stock and wine; spoon 3 teaspoons into six 125 ml (4 fl oz/½ cup) capacity oval moulds. Refrigerate until set.

Lift cooled fish out of pan, reserving cooking liquid. Cut salmon into small pieces; slice scallops. Layer up the fish, prawns and dill in each mould. Pour over a little gelatine mixture as layers build up. Refrigerate until set.

To make dressing, heat oil in a small pan, cook shallot for 2 minutes, add cooking liquid from fish and simmer for 5 minutes. Place saffron threads in a bowl, then pour over the hot fish liquid and leave to cool.

Turn out jellies onto a serving plate. Strain saffron mixture and whisk in cream. Pour a little around each jelly and serve garnished with any remaining prawns and dill.

Serves 6.

CAESAR SALAD

90 ml (3 fl oz/⅓ cup) olive oil
2 cloves garlic, halved
4 thick slices bread
1 cos lettuce
6 anchovy fillets, chopped
30 g (1 oz/¼ cup) grated Parmesan cheese
SOFT EGG DRESSING:
1 egg
5 teaspoons lemon juice
3 tablespoons olive oil
1 teaspoon Worcestershire sauce
¼ teaspoon Dijon mustard
salt and pepper

Place oil in a bowl with garlic; allow to stand for 1 hour, then remove garlic.

Toast bread, remove crusts and cut into squares. Heat garlic-flavoured oil in a frying pan. Add bread cubes and fry until crisp and golden, turning frequently. Lift out croûtons and drain on absorbent kitchen paper.

To assemble salad, tear most of the lettuce into large pieces, reserving a few small inner leaves whole. Arrange whole leaves around edge of a salad bowl. Put torn lettuce in the centre with croûtons, anchovies and Parmesan cheese.

To make dressing, boil egg for 1 minute. Crack open into a bowl, scraping out from the shell. Add remaining ingredients, seasoning to taste with salt and pepper, and whisk until smooth.

Pour dressing over salad and toss gently. Serve immediately

Serves 4.

— STUFFED TOMATO SALAD —

12 firm tomatoes
90 g (3 oz) curd cheese
1 tablespoon single (light) cream
60 g (2 oz) smoked spiced ham, finely chopped
2.5 cm (1 in) piece cucumber, peeled and finely chopped
2 teaspoons chopped fresh dill or chives
a few salad leaves, to serve
1-2 tablespoons Herb Vinaigrette, see page 11
cucumber slices, to garnish

Cut tops off tomatoes with a serrated-edge knife. With the tip of the knife, cut round insides and scoop out seeds with a small spoon. Turn tomato shells upside-down on absorbent kitchen paper to drain.

Put cheese and cream into a bowl and beat until smooth. Stir in chopped ham, cucumber and chopped dill or chives. Spoon into tomatoes shells, then replace lids. In a bowl, toss salad leaves in dressing until well coated, then arrange on 4 plates. Place 3 tomatoes on each plate, and serve garnished with slices of cucumber.

Serves 4.

Variations: Use larger tomatoes and cut in half to give a vandyked edge, or cut the tomatoes into basket shapes.

— SMOKED SALMON NESTS —

2 sheets filo pastry
30 g (1 oz/6 teaspoons) butter, melted
60 g (2 oz) curly endive
2.5 cm (1 in) piece cucumber
125 g (4 oz) smoked salmon
2 tablespoons Lemon Vinaigrette, see page 10

Heat oven to 200C (400F/Gas 6). Cut filo pastry into twelve 8 cm (3½ in) squares. Brush with butter and place in 4 individual Yorkshire pudding tins, putting 3 pieces in each. Gently press into tins, then bake for 10 minutes until crisp and golden. Leave to cool.

Put endive into a bowl. Cut cucumber into short batons and salmon into strips. Add to bowl with dressing and toss well. Pile into pastry cases and serve at once.

Serves 4.

LEEKS À LA GREQUE

500 g (1 lb) young leeks
60 ml (2 fl oz/¼ cup) olive oil
1 onion, finely chopped
3 tomatoes, skinned, seeded and chopped
1 clove garlic, crushed
155 ml (5 fl oz/⅔ cup) dry white wine
12 coriander seeds, slightly crushed
1 bay leaf
pinch cayenne pepper
salt and pepper
2 teaspoons chopped fresh thyme
chopped black olives and thyme, to garnish

Wash and trim leeks. Cut into 5 cm (2 in) lengths, then blanch in a saucepan of boiling water for 2 minutes. Drain and set aside.

Heat 3 tablespoons oil in a large saucepan. Add onion and 1 table-spoon water and cook gently for 8 minutes. Add tomatoes, garlic, wine, coriander seeds, bay leaf and cayenne pepper. Season with salt and pepper and cook for about 15 minutes, or until tomatoes are pulpy. Add leeks and cook un-covered for 10-15 minutes until tender. If sauce is getting dry, add a little water.

Discard bay leaf, then allow mixture to cool. Transfer to a serving dish, sprinkle over thyme and chill until needed.

To serve, drizzle remaining oil over leeks and garnish with chopped olives and thyme.

Serves 4.

— MARINATED MUSHROOMS —

2 tablespoons olive oil
1 shallot, finely chopped
125 g (4 oz) shiitake mushrooms, stalks removed and sliced if large
90 ml (3 fl oz/⅓ cup) dry white wine
125 g (4 oz) button mushrooms, trimmed
125 g (4 oz) oyster mushrooms
1 teaspoon pink peppercorns in brine, drained
1 teaspoon green peppercorns in brine, drained
3 tablespoons walnut oil
½ teaspoon Dijon mustard
salt
1 teaspoon chopped fresh oregano
watercress sprigs, to garnish

Heat olive oil in a frying pan and cook shallot for 2 minutes. Add shiitake mushrooms, sauté for 2-3 minutes, then pour over wine and simmer for 2 minutes. Remove from heat, turn into a bowl and leave to cool.

Slice button mushrooms and halve oyster mushrooms if large. Strain the marinating liquid from shiitake mushrooms into a small bowl. Mix all the mushrooms together in a bowl with peppercorns.

Whisk walnut oil and mustard into cooking liquid and season with salt. Pour over mushrooms and stir together. Sprinkle oregano over the top and leave to marinate for up to 1 hour before serving garnished with watercress.

Serves 4.

———— SMOKED FISH PLATTER ————

2 smoked trout fillets
2 peppered smoked mackerel fillets
3 slices bread, toasted
30 g (1 oz/6 teaspoons) butter
1 teaspoon lemon juice
100 g (3½ oz) can smoked oysters, drained
small lettuce leaves, lemon slices and parsley or dill, to garnish
HORSERADISH SAUCE:
3 tablespoons Greek strained yogurt
2 teaspoons horseradish relish
1 teaspoon lemon juice
2 teaspoons chopped fresh parsley
pepper

Skin trout and mackerel fillets and carefully cut them into small even-sized pieces. Set them aside.

Using a small fancy cutter, cut out 4 rounds from each toast. Beat butter and lemon juice together. Spread a little on the toast rounds. Place a smoked oyster on each buttered toast round.

Arrange the pieces of smoked fish and the oysters on toast on 4 plates. Garnish each plate with a few lettuce leaves, lemon slices and parsley or dill.

Make sauce by mixing ingredients together in a bowl. Spoon into a serving dish and serve with salads.

Serves 4.

— STILTON & WALNUT SALAD —

2 heads chicory
2 heads Little Gem lettuce, shredded
1 large ripe pear
60 g (2 oz) blue Stilton, grated
walnut halves, to garnish
WALNUT DRESSING:
60 g (2 oz/⅓ cup) walnut pieces
4 tablespoons sunflower oil
2 tablespoons lemon juice
2 tablespoons apple juice
salt and pepper

Chop chicory and put into a bowl with the shredded lettuce. Peel and quarter pear, remove core, then cut into small slices. Add to bowl with cheese.

To make the dressing, put ingredients into a blender and work until smooth. Pour over salad and toss together. Divide between 4 plates, and serve garnished with walnuts.

Serves 4.

— JELLIED GAZPACHO SALAD —

500 g (1 lb) tomatoes, skinned, seeded and chopped

1 small onion, chopped

1 clove garlic, crushed

½ teaspoon celery salt

1 teaspoon tomato purée (paste)

1 teaspoon white wine vinegar

3 teaspoons powdered gelatine

salt and pepper

TO FINISH:

7.5 cm (3 in) piece cucumber, peeled and diced

¼ Spanish onion, finely diced

½ green pepper (capsicum), seeded and diced

2 sticks celery, diced

mustard and cress, to garnish

Put tomatoes, onion, garlic, celery salt, tomato purée (paste) and vinegar into a saucepan and simmer until soft and pulpy. Sieve mixture into a measuring jug.

Sprinkle gelatine over 4 table-spoons water in a small bowl and leave to soften for 2-3 minutes. Stand bowl in a saucepan of hot water and stir until dissolved. Allow to cool, then stir into the tomato mixture, making up to 625 ml (20 fl oz/2½ cups) with water if necessary. Season with salt and pepper. Pour into 4 individual 155 ml (5 fl oz/⅔ cup) ring moulds and refrigerate until set.

To turn out, dip each mould into a bowl of hot water for a few seconds, then invert onto a serving plate.

Arrange diced vegetables around each jelly and serve garnished with mustard and cress.

Serves 4.

ITALIAN SEAFOOD SALAD

1 kg (2 lb) fresh mussels, scrubbed and debearded
500 g (1 lb) fresh clams, scrubbed
3 small squid
1 tablespoon extra virgin olive oil
185 g (6 oz) peeled cooked prawns
CAPER DRESSING:
75 ml (2½ fl oz/⅓ cup) extra virgin olive oil
2 tablespoons lemon juice
1 tablespoon chopped fresh parsley
1 clove garlic, finely chopped
1 tablespoon capers, drained
salt and pepper
parsley and lemon wedges, to garnish, if desired

Put mussels into a large saucepan with a cupful of water. Cover, cook over high heat for 5 minutes until mussles open. Remove from heat, discard any which remain closed. Allow to cool slightly.

Remove mussels from shells. Prepare clams in the same way, discarding any that remain closed.

To prepare squid, pull off tentacles and remove transparent bone in body. Remove any skin, then cut tubes into thin slices. Cut off tentacles just in front of eyes and set aside.

Heat oil in a heavy-based frying pan. Add squid rings and tentacles and sauté for about 2 minutes until opaque. Turn into a bowl and add other shellfish.

To make dressing, mix ingredients together in a bowl or screw-top jar. Pour over fish and refrigerate for 2 hours.

Serve garnished with parsley and lemon wedges, if desired.

Serves 4.

CAPONATA

2 aubergines (eggplants)
salt
125 ml (4 fl oz/½ cup) olive oil
1 small onion, chopped
4 sticks celery, chopped
440 g (14 oz) can chopped tomatoes
2-3 tablespoons red wine vinegar
1 tablespoon sugar
1 tablespoon capers, drained
12 green olives, stoned and chopped
1 tablespoon pine nuts, lightly toasted
salt and pepper
parsley sprigs, to garnish

Cut aubergines (eggplants) into small cubes, put into a colander. Sprinkle with salt and set aside to drain for 1 hour.

Meanwhile, heat 2 tablespoons oil in a saucepan, add onion and cook over medium heat for 5 minutes until soft. Add celery and continue to cook for 3 minutes. Stir in tomatoes and juice and simmer, un-covered, for 5 minutes. Add vinegar and sugar and simmer for a further 15 minutes.

Rinse aubergines (eggplants) and dry on absorbent kitchen paper. Heat remaining oil in a large frying pan and cook aubergines (egg-plants), stirring, until tender and golden. Transfer with slotted spoon to tomato sauce. Add capers, olives and pine nuts and season with salt and pepper. Continue to simmer for 2-3 minutes.

Spoon into a serving dish and cool. Serve garnished with parsley.

Serves 6.

Note: This dish tastes better if left in the refrigerator for 24 hours to allow flavours to mingle.

Variation: For a more substantial dish, garnish with flaked tuna fish.

CELERIAC & MUSSELS

750 g (1½ lb) celeriac
2 tablespoons lemon juice
1 kg (2 lb) fresh mussels, scrubbed and de-bearded
2 tablespoons dry white wine
RÉMOULADE SAUCE:
75 ml (2½ fl oz/⅓ cup) Mayonnaise, see page 12
2 teaspoons chopped gherkins
1 teaspoon chopped capers
1 teaspoon chopped fresh parsley
1 teaspoon anchovy paste

Peel celeriac and cut into thin slices. Immediately put into a saucepan half-full of boiling water with lemon juice. Simmer for 4-5 minutes or until just tender. Drain, then cut into thin strips and put into a bowl to cool.

Put mussels into a large saucepan with wine, cover and cook over a high heat for about 5 minutes until mussels open. Remove from heat and discard any which remain closed. Strain mussels, reserving broth. Reserve a few mussels in the shells for garnish. Remove remainder from shells and add to celeriac.

To make sauce, put ingredients into a bowl with 2-3 tablespoons of reserved broth, then mix together to give a consistency of thick cream. Stir into celeriac and mussels.

Spoon into a serving dish or 4 individual dishes and garnish with reserved mussels.

Serves 4.

KIPPER SALAD

3 large natural smoked kippers
2 tablespoons virgin olive oil
60 ml (2 fl oz/¼ cup) lemon juice
1 teaspoon sugar
1 onion, sliced
1 bay leaf
lemon slices and mustard and cress, to garnish

Bone and skin kippers. Slice fillets and put into a glass dish. Pour over the oil and lemon juice. Add the sugar, onion and bay leaf, then mix together. Cover the dish and refrigerate for about 24 hours.

Drain kipper pieces and onion and divide between 4 plates. Serve garnished with lemon slices and mustard and cress.

Serves 4.

— INDONESIAN SEAFOOD SALAD —

375 g (12 oz) unpeeled cooked prawns
1 tablespoon sunflower oil
1 small onion, finely chopped
1 clove garlic, crushed
3 tomatoes, skinned, seeded and chopped
3 teaspoons dark soy sauce
1 teaspoon ground ginger
1 green chilli, seeded and finely chopped
1 tablespoon red wine vinegar
250 g (8 oz) prepared squid, see page 27
red or green pepper (capsicum) strips, to garnish

Peel the prawns, leaving the tail shells intact but discarding the rest of the shells. Set aside prawns.

Heat the oil in a saucepan and cook the onion until soft. Add garlic, tomatoes, soy sauce, ginger, chilli and vinegar and simmer for 5 minutes.

Stir rings of squid, tentacles and prawns into sauce and cook, uncovered, for 5 minutes. Allow seafood to cool in sauce. To serve, divide seafood and sauce between 4 dishes and garnish with strips of pepper (capsicum).

Serves 4.

TOMATO & MOZZARELLA SALAD

2 beefsteak tomatoes
185 g (6 oz) Mozzarella cheese, sliced
1 small purple onion, thinly sliced
salt and pepper
60 ml (2 fl oz/¼ cup) extra virgin olive oil
1 tablespoon fresh basil leaves
1 tablespoon pine nuts

Slice the tomatoes and arrange with slices of cheese, on 4 plates. Arrange onion rings on top. Season with salt and pepper, then drizzle oil over the top.

Scatter over the basil and pine nuts and serve at once.

Serves 4.

— SPINACH & BACON SALAD —

125 g (4 oz) young spinach leaves, washed and trimmed

60 g (2 oz) button mushrooms, sliced

3 thick slices bread, crusts removed

60 ml (2 fl oz/¼ cup) sunflower oil

1 clove garlic, crushed

185 g (6 oz) streaky bacon, rinds removed and chopped

2 tablespoons white wine vinegar

pepper

Shred spinach and put into a salad bowl with the mushrooms.

Cut bread into small squares. Heat oil in a frying pan, add bread and garlic and fry until golden. Remove with a slotted spoon and drain on absorbent kitchen paper. Wipe out pan with absorbent kitchen paper, then add bacon and cook for about 5 minutes until crisp and golden.

Pour bacon and any fat over spinach. Add vinegar to pan with a few grinds of pepper, bring to the boil, then immediately pour over salad and toss. Scatter over the crôutons and serve at once.

Serves 6.

AVOCADO CRAB LOUIS

2 avocados

1 tablespoon lemon juice

250 g (8 oz) white crabmeat, well drained
if canned and flaked

fresh chervil sprigs, to garnish

brown bread and butter, to serve

SEAFOOD SAUCE:

60 ml (2 fl oz/¼ cup) Mayonnaise, see
page 12

1 tablespoon tomato ketchup (sauce)

½ teaspoon Worcestershire sauce

60 ml (2 fl oz/¼ cup) single (light) cream

2 teaspoons lemon juice

1 teaspoon dry sherry

pinch cayenne pepper

Halve the avocados, remove the
stones, then peel. Slice and brush
with lemon juice to prevent dis-
coloration. Then arrange the slices
on 4 plates.

To make sauce, mix ingredients
together in a bowl, then fold in
crabmeat.

Divide the crabmeat mixture
between the plates, then garnish
each with sprigs of fresh chervil.
Serve the salads with brown bread
and butter.

Serves 4.

— SMOKED CHICKEN EXOTICA —

3 smoked chicken breasts (fillets), skinned and boned
1 star fruit (carambola), sliced and pips removed
1 papaya, peeled, seeded and sliced
2 fresh figs, quartered
½ mango, peeled and diced
1 tablespoon chopped stem ginger, to garnish
MANGO DRESSING:
½ mango, peeled
60 ml (2 fl oz/¼ cup) sunflower oil
1 tablespoon sherry vinegar
pinch mixed spice

Slice chicken and arrange on 4 plates with slices of star fruit, papaya, figs and diced mango.

To make the dressing, put ingredients into a blender and work until smooth. Drizzle over salads or place in the centres. Garnish with ginger.

Serves 4.

CHICKEN LIVER TIÈDE

1 potato, weighing about 185 g (6 oz)
185 g (6 oz) broccoli flowerets
2 small courgettes (zucchini), sliced
250 g (8 oz) chicken livers, washed
60 ml (2 fl oz/¼ cup) virgin olive oil
salt and pepper
2 tablespoons sherry vinegar
2 shallots, thinly sliced, to garnish

Cut the potato into 0.5 cm (¼ in) matchsticks. Put into a saucepan of water, bring to the boil and cook for 3 minutes. Add broccoli and cook for 2 minutes. Add courgettes (zucchini) to pan and simmer a further 1 minute. Drain vegetables in a colander.

Cut membranes from chicken livers, then dry livers on absorbent kitchen paper. Heat oil in a frying pan, add livers and season with salt and pepper. Cook for 5 minutes, stirring constantly; they should be soft and pink inside. Remove from the pan with slotted spoon.

Divide vegetables between 4 plates, slice the livers and scatter over vegetables.

Add vinegar to pan, warm quickly, then pour over the salads. Scatter over slices of shallot and serve at once.

Serves 4 as a starter.

SOLE WITH CAPERS

2 sole fillets, each weighing about 250 g (8 oz), skinned
90 ml (3 fl oz/⅓ cup) dry white wine
2 heads chicory, chopped
1 bunch watercress, trimmed
2 teaspoons capers
MARINADE:
1 lemon
60 ml (2 fl oz/¼ cup) virgin oil
6 teaspoons lemon juice
1 tablespoon chopped fresh parsley
1 shallot, finely chopped
salt and pepper

To prepare marinade, remove peel from lemon, using a zester, and cut into shreds. Squeeze the juice from the lemon and put into a bowl with other ingredients.

Cut fish fillets in half lengthwise, then across into thin strips. Place in a frying pan with wine and poach for 2 minutes. Lift out of pan with a slotted spoon, place in marinade and leave to marinate for 10 minutes.

Arrange chicory and watercress on 4 plates. Remove fish from marinade and divide between plates.

Reduce poaching liquid to 4 tablespoons by boiling rapidly. Add capers and marinade, then warm together. Quickly pour over the salads and serve at once while the dressing is still hot.

Serves 4 as a starter.

LOBSTER & ASPARAGUS SALAD

1 cooked lobster, weighing about 750 g (1½ lb)
250 g (8 oz) fresh asparagus, cut into 5 cm (2 in) pieces
heart of 1 spring cabbage, weighing about 185 g (6 oz), shredded
tarragon sprigs, to garnish
TARRAGON DRESSING:
3 tablespoons virgin olive oil
3 teaspoons tarragon vinegar
2 teaspoons chopped fresh tarragon, if desired
salt and pepper

To prepare lobster, remove large claws and pinchers. Crack open claws; remove meat, trying to keep it in chunks. Using point of a sharp knife, split lobster into 2 pieces from head to tail. Starting at tail, remove meat, discarding brown feathery gills. Remove liver to use in another recipe. Remove dark coral if there is any and reserve. Extract meat from body with a skewer. Slice the tail meat.

Cook asparagus in a steamer for 7 minutes. Add cabbage and steam for a further 2 minutes. Arrange vegetables and lobster meat on 4 plates.

To make the dressing, mix all the ingredients in a bowl or screw-top jar, then drizzle over the salads. Garnish with lobster coral and sprigs of tarragon. Serve at once.

Serves 4 as a starter.

GOAT'S CHEESE SALAD

1 head radicchio

4 slices granary bread

two 125 g (4 oz) whole goat's cheeses

2 sticks celery, chopped

30 g (1 oz) walnut halves, chopped

celery leaves, to garnish

WALNUT GARLIC DRESSING:

3 tablespoons walnut oil

3 teaspoons red wine vinegar

1 clove garlic, crushed

salt and pepper

To make dressing, mix ingredients together in a bowl or screw-top jar.

Divide radicchio leaves and put into a bowl. Pour dressing onto the leaves and toss together, then arrange on 4 plates.

Toast bread; cut out 4 rounds. Cut each cheese in half horizontally and trim off end crusts. Place a portion of cheese on each round of toast, then place under medium-hot grill for about 3-4 minutes until golden. Transfer to plates and scatter over the chopped celery and walnuts. Garnish with celery leaves and serve at once.

Serves 4 as a starter.

— PRAWNS WITH MANGE TOUT —

12 raw Mediterranean (king) prawns

125 g (4 oz) mange tout (snow peas), trimmed

3 tablespoons virgin olive oil

1 tablespoon finely shredded fresh root ginger

juice and grated peel of 1 lime

3 teaspoons soy sauce

Peel prawns, leaving tail shells on. Make a small incision along spines. Remove black spinal cords from prawns. Cook mange tout (snow peas) in boiling water for 1 minute, drain and arrange on 4 plates.

Heat the oil in a large frying pan, add prawns and ginger and cook gently for 5 minutes, turning them once.

Add lime juice, peel and soy sauce; cook for 1 minute. Arrange the prawns on the mange tout (snow peas), then pour over dressing. Serve at once.

Serves 4 as a starter.

— CALVES LIVER BALSAMICO —

few batavia leaves
few lollo rosso leaves
60 g (2 oz) lamb's lettuce
60 ml (2 fl oz/¼ cup) extra virgin olive oil
2 large slices calves liver, weighing 250 g (8 oz), cut into ribbons
1 tablespoon shredded fresh sage leaves
2 tablespoons balsamico vinegar
salt and pepper
pine nuts, to garnish

Tear salad leaves into smaller pieces and arrange on 4 plates.

Heat oil in a frying pan, add liver and sage and cook for 2-3 minutes, stirring constantly. Remove with a slotted spoon and divide between the plates.

Pour vinegar into pan, season with salt and pepper and warm through. Spoon over the salads and serve garnished with pine nuts.

Serves 4 as a starter.

—— DUCK WITH KUMQUATS ——

90 g (3 oz) young spinach leaves, trimmed
4 duck breast fillets, skinned
155 ml (5 fl oz/⅔ cup) dry white wine
pinch ground ginger
8 coriander seeds, crushed
salt and pepper
12 kumquats, sliced
3 tablespoons hazelnut oil
2 teaspoons lemon juice
pomegranate seeds, to garnish

Wash and dry spinach and arrange on 4 plates.

Put duck breasts into a frying pan and pour over the wine. Add ginger and coriander. Season with salt and pepper. Cover pan and simmer for 10 minutes until duck is tender. Add kumquats and simmer for 1 minute. Remove duck and kumquats from pan with a slotted spoon and set aside.

Simmer the liquid in the pan until reduced to 60 ml (2 fl oz/¼ cup). Stir in oil and lemon juice and warm through.

Slice the duck and arrange on the plates with the kumquats. Pour over dressing, then serve garnished with pomegranate seeds.

Serves 4 as a main course.

— LAMB & NOODLE SQUASH —

1 boneless, rolled saddle joint of lamb, weighing about 750 g (1½ lb)
1 clove garlic, slivered
salt and pepper
rosemary sprigs
1 noodle (spaghetti) squash, weighing about 750 g (1½ lb)
cooked frozen peas and rosemary sprigs, to garnish
RED PEPPER DRESSING:
1 small red pepper (capsicum), roasted and skinned, see page 110
1 teaspoon sherry vinegar
3 tablespoons virgin olive oil

Preheat oven to 200C (400F/Gas 6). With a sharp knife, make incisions in the lamb and push in slivers of garlic. Season lamb with salt and pepper, then place in a roasting tin with sprigs of rosemary. Cook in the oven for 40 minutes.

Meanwhile, cut the squash in half, discard the seeds, then place in a roasting pan, cut side down, with enough water to come halfway up sides of pan. Simmer for 15-20 minutes until squash is tender. Remove from the pan and scoop out the centre into a colander. Drain.

To make the dressing, remove core and seeds from the pepper and put the flesh into a blender or food processor with the vinegar and oil, work until smooth. Season with salt and pepper and set aside.

Remove lamb from oven and stand for 5 minutes. Divide squash between 6 plates. Slice lamb and arrange on the plates. Spoon over dressing and garnish with a few peas and sprigs of rosemary.

Serves 6 as a main course.

PEPPERY CHICKEN SALAD

60 g (2 oz) lollo rosso or radicchio
¼ head curly endive
60 g (2 oz) lamb's lettuce
4 tomatoes, skinned
4 chicken breasts (fillets), skinned
315 ml (10 fl oz/1¼ cups) dry white wine
salt and pepper
1½ teaspoons green peppercorns in brine, drained
75 ml (2½ fl oz/⅓ cup) single (light) cream

Wash and dry salad leaves, tear any large ones into smaller pieces, then divide between 4 plates. Cut each tomato into 8 wedges, remove seeds, then arrange over the lettuce leaves on the plates.

Put chicken breasts into a frying pan, pour over wine and season with salt and pepper. Poach for 15 minutes until chicken is tender. Lift out of pan with slotted spoon, place on a chopping board and slice.

Add the peppercorns to the cooking liquid, then boil rapidly until liquid is reduced to 5 tablespoons. Stir in cream and warm through. Arrange the chicken on the salad, pour over cream dressing and serve immediately.

Serves 4 as a main course.

HOT SAUSAGE SALAD

185 g (6 oz) finely shredded red cabbage
185 g (6 oz) finely shredded white cabbage
1 cooking apple
1 teaspoon lemon juice
1 pork boiling ring sausage
1 tablespoon chopped fresh parsley, to garnish
MUSTARD MAYONNAISE:
2 tablespoons Mayonnaise, see page 12
2 tablespoons low fat soft cheese
2 teaspoons wholegrain mustard
2 teaspoons apple juice
salt and pepper

Put shredded cabbage into a bowl and mix together. Grate apple, toss with lemon juice, then add to cabbage.

Cook sausage according to packet directions. Meanwhile, make mayonnaise by mixing ingredients together in a bowl. Stir into cabbage, then spoon onto 4 plates.

Slice cooked sausage and arrange over salad. Garnish with parsley.

Serves 4 as a main course.

— ORIENTAL CHICKEN SALAD —

2 cooked chicken breasts (fillets), skinned
185 g (6 oz) beansprouts, trimmed
125 g (4 oz) button mushrooms, sliced
1 yellow pepper (capsicum), seeded and diced
3 spring onions, chopped
2 carrots, cut into matchsticks
½ quantity Chinese Dressing, see page 15
toasted sesame seeds and radish flowers, to garnish

Shred chicken and put into a bowl with beansprouts, mushrooms, pepper (capsicum), spring onions, and carrots; mix together.

Pour the dressing over the salad, toss together, then transfer to a serving dish. Sprinkle over the sesame seeds and garnish with radish flowers. Serve at once.

Serves 4.

THAI SEAFOOD SALAD

250 g (8 oz) monkfish, skinned and cubed
4 scallops, thawed if frozen
250 g (8 oz) salmon steak, skinned and cubed
8 raw Mediterranean (king) prawns
5 cm (2 in) piece fresh ginger, shredded
2 bulbs lemon grass, peeled and chopped
spring onion curls, to garnish
MARINADE:
juice of 1 lime
4 teaspoons light soy sauce
2 teaspoons chopped fresh mint
3 teaspoons chopped fresh coriander
1 clove garlic, crushed
WILD RICE SALAD:
45 g (1½ oz/3 tablespoons) wild rice
2.5 cm (1 in) piece fresh ginger, halved
45 g (1½ oz/3 tablespoons) long grain rice
1 tablespoon light sesame oil
6 coriander seeds, crushed

Put all seafood onto a plate, scatter ginger and lemon grass over the top.

Place an upturned saucer in a wok, add 1 cupful of water. Stand plate on saucer. Cover and steam for 5-6 minutes until the seafood is cooked. Or, use a steamer.

To make marinade, mix ingredients together in large bowl. Add cooked fish with 2 tablespoons of cooking juices. Stir gently, then leave to marinate for at least 1 hour.

To make rice salad, put wild rice and ginger into a saucepan of simmering water and cook for 30 minutes. Add long grain rice, cook a further 20 minutes until tender.

Drain rice and discard the ginger. Stir in sesame oil and coriander seeds. Divide rice between 4 plates, arrange fish on top and spoon over marinade. Garnish with spring onion curls.

Serves 4.

SALAD NIÇOISE

125 g (4 oz) thin green beans, trimmed

6 tomatoes, quartered

½ cucumber, peeled and diced

1 red pepper (capsicum), seeded and sliced

6 spring onions, chopped

220 g (7 oz) can tuna fish, drained and flaked

90 g (3 oz) black olives, stoned

1 tablespoon chopped fresh parsley

3 eggs, hard-boiled

60 g (2 oz) can anchovies, drained

MUSTARD VINAIGRETTE DRESSING:

60 ml (2 fl oz/¼ cup) extra virgin olive oil

1 tablespoon red wine vinegar

1 tablespoon lemon juice

¼ teaspoon Dijon mustard

salt and pepper

Cook beans in a saucepan of water for 5-6 minutes, until just tender. Drain, rinse under cold water, then cut into 4 cm (1½ in) lengths. Put into a bowl with tomatoes, cucumber, red pepper (capsicum), spring onions, tuna fish and olives. Mix together.

To make dressing, mix ingredients together in a bowl or screw-top jar, add to the salad with the parsley and toss gently. Quarter the hard-boiled eggs and arrange on the salad. Cut anchovy fillets in half lengthwise and arrange in criss-cross patterns on top of salad.

Serves 4.

CORONATION CHICKEN

2 kg (4 lb) chicken, cooked

paprika

1 carrot, sliced and cut into flowers and 1 stick celery, cut into thin strips, to garnish

CURRY MAYONNAISE:

60 ml (2 fl oz/¼ cup) Mayonnaise, see page 12

2 tablespoons lemon juice

2 tablespoons single (light) cream

5 tablespoons natural yogurt

1 teaspoon tomato purée (paste)

1 teaspoon curry paste

2 tablespoons mango chutney

Remove the chicken meat from bones, discarding skin and bones. Divide meat into neat pieces and place on a serving platter.

To make the Curry Mayonnaise, put all the ingredients into a blender or food processor and work until smooth. Pour over the chicken and dust with paprika. Serve garnished with carrot flowers and celery.

Serves 6.

CHINESE LEAF SALAD

500 g (1 lb) Chinese leaves, chopped
6 spring onions, shredded
125 g (4 oz) sweetcorn, thawed if frozen
125 g (4 oz) mange tout (snow peas)
1 red chilli, seeded and finely sliced
3 eggs
a few drops light soy sauce
3 teaspoons sunflower oil
9 teaspoons sesame seeds, toasted
1 quantity Chinese Dressing, see page 15
red chilli flowers, to garnish

In a serving dish, arrange Chinese leaves, spring onions and sweetcorn. Blanch mange tout (snow peas) in a saucepan of boiling water for 30 seconds. Drain, cut in half, then add to salad with the chilli.

Break 1 egg into a bowl, beat in a few drops of soy sauce. Heat 1 teaspoon oil in a small omelette pan, pour in beaten egg. Cook until set, slide omelette onto a plate and sprinkle over 3 teaspoons sesame seeds; roll up like a Swiss roll and leave to cool. Repeat the process with the other 2 eggs and sesame seeds to make a total of 3 omelettes rolled and cooled.

Pour the dressing over the salad and toss gently. Slice omelettes into 2.5 cm (1 in) pieces, arrange over the salad and serve garnished with red chilli flowers.

Serves 4.

MALAYSIAN SALAD

250 g (8 oz) white cabbage, shredded
125 g (4 oz) thin green beans, cut into
2.5 cm (1 in) lengths
½ small cauliflower, divided into flowerets
125 g (4 oz) beansprouts, trimmed
½ cucumber
coriander leaves, to garnish
PEANUT SAUCE:
30 g (1 oz) desiccated coconut
155 ml (5 fl oz/⅔ cup) boiling water
3 tablespoons peanut butter
2 teaspoons soy sauce
juice of ½ lime
¼ teaspoon chilli powder

To make sauce, place coconut in a bowl, pour over boiling water and leave to soak for 15 minutes.

Bring a large saucepan of water to the boil, add cabbage, beans and cauliflower and simmer for 2-3 minutes. Drain vegetables thoroughly, arrange on a platter or 4 individual plates. Scatter over beansprouts. Cut strips of skin from cucumber with a canelle knife, then slice the cucumber and arrange over salad.

Strain coconut milk into a bowl, discard the coconut, and add remaining sauce ingredients; mix well. Spoon onto centre of salad or serve separately. Garnish the salad with coriander leaves.

Serves 4.

— STUFFED EGG TARA SALAD —

6 large eggs, hard-boiled
125 g (4 oz) taramasalata
6 tomatoes, finely diced
½ cucumber, finely diced
1 small green pepper (capsicum), seeded and finely diced
1 avocado
½ quantity Lemon Vinaigrette, see page 10
black or red lumpfish and dill sprigs, to garnish

Halve the eggs crossways, remove yolks and put into a bowl. Cut a sliver off the end of each egg white so they will stand up.

Add taramasalata to egg yolks and beat together. Spoon into the egg whites.

In a bowl, mix tomatoes, cucumber and pepper (capsicum). Peel avocado, cut in half and remove stone. Dice flesh and add to the bowl with the dressing; mix gently. Spoon onto a serving dish, then arrange the eggs on top. Serve garnished with a little lumpfish on each egg, and sprigs of dill.

Serves 4.

PASTA PESTO SALAD

250 g (8 oz) orzo (rice-shaped pasta)

250 g (8 oz) cherry tomatoes, quartered

30 g (1 oz) pine nuts, lightly toasted

basil sprigs, to garnish

PESTO DRESSING:

30 g (1 oz) fresh basil leaves

2 cloves garlic, peeled

30 g (1 oz) pine nuts

3 tablespoons virgin olive oil

30 g (1 oz/¼ cup) grated Parmesan cheese

3 tablespoons single (light) cream

Cook pasta in boiling salted water until just tender. Drain, rinse under cold water and drain again. Put into a bowl with the tomatoes.

To make the dressing, wash and dry basil leaves, then put into a blender or food processor with garlic, pine nuts and oil and work until smooth. Turn into a bowl, and beat in Parmesan cheese and cream. Stir into the pasta, then transfer to a serving dish. Serve the salad sprinkled with toasted pine nuts and garnished with a few sprigs of basil.

Serves 4.

—— ITALIAN SALAMI SALAD ——

470 g (15 oz) can haricot or cannellini
beans, drained

1 bulb fennel, finely sliced

1 small green pepper (capsicum), seeded
and diced

125 g (4 oz) Italian salami, sliced

basil leaves, tomato wedges and black
olives, to garnish

GARLIC DRESSING:

3 tablespoons extra virgin olive oil

1 tablespoon white wine vinegar

1 clove garlic, crushed with salt

pepper

Put beans, fennel and green pepper
(capsicum) into a bowl. Cut salami
slices into quarters and add to the
salad.

To make the dressing, mix ingredients together in a bowl or screw-
top jar. Pour over the salad and toss
together gently.

Spoon onto a serving dish and
serve garnished with basil, tomato
wedges and olives.

Serves 4.

STROGANOFF SALAD

375 g (12 oz) cold, rare cooked beef
250 g (8 oz) button mushrooms, sliced
6 spring onions, chopped or shredded
1 red pepper (capsicum), seeded and sliced
shredded lettuce, to serve
SOUR CREAM DRESSING:
155 ml (5 fl oz/⅔ cup) thick sour cream
1 tablespoon horseradish sauce
2 teaspoons lemon juice
salt and pepper

Cut the beef into thin strips and put into a bowl with the mushrooms, onions and pepper (capsicum).

To make the dressing, mix ingredients together in a bowl. Pour over the salad and toss gently. Line a serving dish with shredded lettuce and spoon salad on top.

Serves 4.

—— SPANISH PAELLA SALAD ——

2 tablespoons olive oil
1 onion, chopped
1 clove garlic, crushed
375 g (12 oz/ 2 cups) arborio (risotto) rice
pinch saffron threads
750 ml (24 fl oz/3 cups) hot chicken stock
250 g (8 oz) tomatoes, skinned, seeded and chopped
125 g (4 oz) cooked frozen peas
2 cooked skinned chicken breasts (fillets), diced
185 g (6 oz) chorizo sausage, skinned and sliced
1 red or green pepper (capsicum), seeded and sliced
stuffed olives, to garnish
PAPRIKA LEMON DRESSING:
3 tablespoons extra virgin olive oil
1 tablespoon lemon juice
½ teaspoon paprika
salt and pepper

Put oil in a large saucepan, add onion and garlic and cook gently for 5 minutes until soft. Stir in rice and cook for 2 minutes.

Stir in the saffron threads and hot stock and simmer until rice is tender and all liquid has been absorbed. Remove from the heat, transfer to a bowl and allow to cool completely.

To make the dressing, mix all the ingredients together in a bowl or screw-top jar.

Add the skinned chopped tomatoes, peas, chicken, sausage and pepper (capsicum) to rice. Pour the dressing over the salad, stir gently and serve garnished with stuffed olives.

Serves 4.

EGGS TONNATO

6 large eggs, hard-boiled
1 canned pimento, cut into strips
60 g (2 oz) anchovies, drained
dill sprigs, to garnish
TONNATO SAUCE:
1 quantity Mayonnaise, see page 12
100 g (3½ oz) can tuna fish, drained
1 tablespoon lemon juice
1 tablespoon single (light) cream or natural yogurt
1 teaspoon capers, drained and chopped

To make sauce, put mayonnaise into a blender or food processor with tuna fish, lemon juice and single (light) cream or natural yogurt and work until smooth. Stir in the capers.

Halve eggs lengthwise and arrange on 4 plates. Spoon the sauce over the eggs and decorate with strips of pimento. Halve the anchovy fillets, then curl them round and place between the eggs. Serve the eggs garnished with sprigs of dill.

Serves 4.

— PASTA & PRAWN SALAD —

250 g (8 oz) pasta shells
375 g (12 oz) peeled cooked prawns
125 g (4 oz) smoked salmon, cut into strips
tarragon sprigs, to garnish
HERB DRESSING:
3 tablespoons virgin olive oil
1 tablespoon lemon juice
1 tablespoon tomato juice
1 tablespoon chopped fresh parsley
1 tablespoon chopped fresh tarragon
salt and pepper

Cook pasta in boiling salted water until just tender. Drain, rinse under cold water and drain again. Put into a bowl with prawns and salmon.

To make the dressing, mix ingredients together in a bowl or screw-top jar. Pour over the salad, toss gently, then transfer to a serving dish. Serve garnished with sprigs of tarragon.

Serves 4.

— BARBECUED STEAK SALAD —

four 185 g (6 oz) fillet steaks
mixed salad leaves
cherry tomatoes, to garnish
MARINADE:
60 ml (2 fl oz/¼ cup) sunflower oil
2 tablespoons red wine vinegar
1 tablespoon tomato purée (paste)
2 teaspoons Worcestershire sauce
1 teaspoon Dijon mustard
1 clove garlic, crushed
½ teaspoon paprika
salt and pepper
AVOCADO DRESSING:
1 ripe avocado
juice of 1 lemon
60 ml (2 fl oz/¼ cup) virgin olive oil
1 clove garlic, crushed
60 ml (2 fl oz/¼ cup) single (light) cream

To make the marinade, put all the ingredients into a dish and mix together. Add the steaks, turn to coat then leave for 1 hour.

To make the dressing, halve the avocado, remove stone and scoop out flesh. Place in blender or food processor with remaining ingredients and work until smooth. Season with salt and pepper.

Arrange salad leaves on 4 plates. Either cook steaks on a barbecue or under a hot grill for 6-8 minutes, turning them once. Transfer cooked steaks to a board, slice them into strips and arrange on the plates. Spoon over dressing. Serve garnished with cherry tomatoes.

Serves 4.

Note: The dressing should be used within 2 hours of being made.

PINK TROUT SALAD

2 large pink trout, cleaned
salt and pepper
a little oil
4 carrots
2 courgettes (zucchini)
15 cm (6 in) piece cucumber
½ carton alfalfa sprouts
1 Webb's lettuce, separated into leaves
tarragon sprigs and nasturtium flowers, to garnish
TARRAGON VINAIGRETTE:
½ quantity Vinaigrette Dressing, see page 10
3 teaspoons freshly chopped tarragon

Season trout with salt and pepper and brush with a little oil. Cook under a preheated grill for 10-15 minutes, until fish flakes when tested, turning once. Allow to cool.

Using a potato peeler, pare thin slices off the carrots, discarding centres, and put into a bowl.

Cut courgettes diagonally to give large, thin slices. Blanch in a saucepan of boiling water for 1 minute. Drain, rinse under cold water and drain again. Add to the carrots.

Using a canelle knife, cut strips of peel from cucumber and discard. Cut the cucumber in half lengthwise, then slice across. Add to the bowl with the alfalfa sprouts.

To make the dressing, mix ingredients together in a bowl or screwtop jar. Pour over salad, toss gently, divide between 4 plates. Arrange lettuce leaves on the plates. Skin and bone trout. Cut flesh into neat pieces and arrange on the salad. Serve garnished with sprigs of tarragon and nasturtium flowers.

Serves 4.

HERRINGSALAT

4 fresh herrings, cleaned, scaled and
backbone removed

2 pickled gherkins, diced

250 g (8 oz) cooked potatoes, diced

½ bunch spring onions, chopped

250 g (8 oz) cooked beetroot, sliced

chives, to garnish

CIDER MARINADE:

125 ml (4 fl oz/½ cup) cider vinegar

125 ml (4 fl oz/½ cup) water

2 tablespoons sugar

1 small onion, chopped

1 bay leaf

good pinch pepper

good pinch allspice

YOGURT MAYONNAISE DRESSING:

6 tablespoons natural yogurt

2 tablespoons Mayonnaise, see page 12

Cut herring fillets into 5 cm (2 in)
pieces and put into a glass dish.

To prepare the marinade,
combine ingredients in a saucepan
and bring to the boil. Simmer for 1
minute, then leave to cool. Pour
over herrings, and marinate overnight or for at least 6 hours.

Drain herrings from marinade
and put into a bowl with gherkins,
potatoes and spring onions. To
make the dressing, mix ingredients
together, then stir into salad.

Arrange sliced beetroot around
edge of serving dish, spoon salad in
centre and garnish with chives.

Serves 4.

— SMOKED MACKEREL SALAD —

500 g (1 lb) new potatoes
1 tablespoon olive oil
4 smoked mackerel fillets
½ cucumber, peeled
parsley sprigs, to garnish
MUSTARD DRESSING:
2 tablespoons sunflower oil
1 tablespoon wholegrain mustard
1 tablespoon lemon juice

In a saucepan of boiling water, cook potatoes in their skins until tender; drain. When cool enough to handle, remove skins, slice potatoes thickly, or quarter. Put into a bowl and toss with olive oil.

Remove skin from mackerel and discard. Break fish into pieces and add to potatoes. Cut cucumber in half crosswise; dice one half and add to salad.

To make the dressing, mix ingredients together in a bowl or screw-top jar. Stir into the salad, then spoon onto a serving dish. Using an apple corer, remove centre from remaining piece of cucumber and discard. Slice cucumber. Serve the salad garnished with cucumber slices and parsley.

Serves 4.

DRESSED CRAB

500 g (1 lb) cooked crab
1 teaspoon lemon juice
1 tablespoon Mayonnaise, see page 12
30 g (1 oz/½ cup) fresh breadcrumbs
salt and pepper
1 egg, hard-boiled
1 tablespoon chopped fresh parsley
lettuce leaves and lemon slices, to garnish
extra mayonnaise, to serve

Hold crab firmly, twist off two claws and legs. Pull body section from shell, discarding feathery gills, the greyish-white stomach sac behind the head and any green matter.

Using a teaspoon, scrape into a bowl all brown meat inside shell. Discard inner membrane attached on either side. Press natural dark line on underside of shell to break along the line neatly; discard the broken inner shell. Wash and dry the main shell.

Snap legs in half by bending backwards at joint. Using a hammer, gently crack all shells; scrape white meat into a second bowl, using a skewer to get into crevices. Discard any bits of shell. Crack large claws, remove meat and add to bowl.

Cut body section in half, pick out white meat from honeycomb structure and add to bowl.

To dress the crab, mix brown meat with lemon juice, mayonnaise and breadcrumbs and season with salt and pepper. Flake white meat with fork. Spoon brown mixture in a line in centre of shell. Carefully place white meat on either side.

Separate hard-boiled egg; sieve yolk and chop white. Cover dark meat with egg yolk, sprinkle a line of egg white on either side of this, then a line of parsley. Garnish with lemon slices and lettuce and serve with mayonnaise.

Serves 1.

CHEF'S SALAD

½ iceberg lettuce
½ Webb's lettuce
4 sticks celery, sliced
½ bunch radishes, sliced
185 g (6 oz) cold cooked chicken
125 g (4 oz) sliced ham
125 g (4 oz) Emmental cheese
BLUE CHEESE DRESSING:
3 tablespoons natural yogurt
3 tablespoons Mayonnaise, see page 12
60 g (2 oz) Danish blue or Roquefort cheese, rinded and crumbled
1 teaspoon lemon juice

Shred iceberg lettuce, tear the Webb's into smaller pieces and put into a salad bowl with the celery and radishes. Cut the chicken, ham and cheese into strips and add to the salad.

To make the dressing, put ingredients into a blender or food processor and work until smooth. Pour over salad and toss gently to coat all the leaves.

Serves 4.

— GERMAN SAUSAGE SALAD —

two 200 g (7 oz) small sticks German sausage, such as salami, bierwurst or Bavarian ham sausage
½ Webb's or iceberg lettuce, shredded
1 red pepper (capsicum), seeded and diced
1 green pepper (capsicum), seeded and diced
1 large head chicory, thinly sliced
½ cucumber, diced
1 quantity Vinaigrette Dressing, see page 10
1 teaspoon poppy seeds, to garnish

Remove skins from the sausages and dice. Put lettuce into a glass serving bowl, scatter over half the diced sausage. Add a layer of peppers, then remaining diced sausage. Add chicory and cucumber, then pour over dressing.

Serve sprinkled with poppy seeds.

Serves 4-6.

—— MARINATED BEEF SALAD ——

500 g (1 lb) piece rump steak	
½ head Chinese leaves	
1 large carrot	
2 spring onions, thinly sliced	
1 tomato, to garnish	
TERIYAKI MARINADE:	
6 tablespoons dry sherry	
3 tablespoons soy sauce	
1 tablespoon red wine vinegar	
2 tablespoons clear honey	
1 clove garlic, crushed	
1 teaspoon ground ginger	

To make the marinade, put all the ingredients into a bowl and mix together. Add beef, turn to coat with marinade. Cover and leave to marinate in the refrigerator over-night, turning meat once.

Preheat oven to 220C (425F/Gas 7). Drain the meat, put into an ovenproof dish, and cook in the oven for 25 minutes. Remove from oven, pour the juices into a jug, and leave to cool.

Arrange Chinese leaves on a platter. Place cooled meat, cut-side down on a board, slice downwards to give oval-shaped slices, then arrange these on the leaves. Skim fat from reserved cooking juices and discard. Drizzle juices over meat.

Using a potato peeler, cut thin ribbons from outside of carrot, discarding centre. Cut these ribbons into fine strips. Scatter the strips around the edge of the dish.

Scatter spring onions over the meat. With a sharp knife, cut peel from tomato and gently roll up to make a rose to garnish the centre of the salad.

Serves 4.

SALMAGUNDI

185 g (6 oz) thin green beans, trimmed
2 hard-boiled eggs, chopped
2 tablespoons chopped fresh parsley
60 g (2 oz) can anchovies, drained and chopped
½ cucumber, diced
1 tablespoon snipped chives
6 spring onions, chopped
3 tomatoes, seeded and chopped
1 lettuce, shredded
250 g (8 oz) cold cooked chicken, diced
125 g (4 oz) cooked ham, diced
250 g (8 oz) cooked new potatoes, sliced
small jar pickled red cabbage, drained
1 tablespoon capers, drained
1 quantity Vinaigrette Dressing, see page 10
borage or nasturtium flowers, to garnish

Cook beans in a saucepan of boiling water for 6-8 minutes, until tender.

Drain, rinse under cold water, then cut into 5 cm (2 in) lengths with a sharp knife.

In a bowl, mix together chopped eggs, parsley and anchovies. In a second bowl, mix together cucumber and chives. In a third bowl, mix together spring onions and tomatoes.

Arrange shredded lettuce on a platter. Spoon the 3 mixtures on top of lettuce leaves with the diced chicken, ham, potatoes, red cabbage and green beans.

Scatter the capers over the top of the salad, then drizzle over the vinaigrette dressing. Garnish with borage or nasturtium flowers and serve at once.

Serves 4.

SAFFRON RICE RING

30 g (1 oz/6 teaspoons) butter

4 cardamom pods

3 cloves

5 cm (2 in) piece cinnamon stick

250 g (8 oz/1¼ cups) basmati rice

500 ml (16 fl oz/2 cups) hot chicken stock

good pinch saffron threads

125 g (4 oz) frozen petit pois

salt and pepper

3 tablespoons single (light) cream

mint sprigs and peeled prawns,

to garnish

FILLING:

250 g (8 oz) peeled cooked prawns

½ cucumber, diced

60 ml (2 fl oz/¼ cup) natural yogurt

2 teaspoons chopped fresh mint

pinch cayenne pepper

In a large saucepan, melt butter, add cardamoms, cloves and cinnamon stick and fry for 1 minute. Stir in rice and cook for 1 minute.

Gradually stir in hot chicken stock, keeping it simmering as it is added. Simmer rice for 15 minutes.

Meanwhile, put saffron into a cup, pour on 2 tablespoons hot water. Stir into rice with peas and continue to cook for 2 minutes. Remove from the heat and season to taste with salt and pepper.

Remove cardamoms, cloves and cinnamon stick, then stir in cream. Spoon rice into a 1.25 litre (2 pint/ 5 cup) ring mould, pressing down with the back of spoon. Cool, then refrigerate for 30 minutes.

Invert rice ring onto a plate. To make filling, mix all the ingredients together in a bowl, then spoon into centre of rice ring. Serve garnished with sprigs of mint and prawns.

Serves 4 as a main course or
6 as a side salad.

TONNO CON FAGIOLI

470 g (15 oz) can cannellini or borlotti
beans, drained

440 g (14 oz) can flageolets (green kidney
beans), drained

½ purple onion, sliced

salt and pepper

two 220 g (7 oz) cans tuna fish, drained

2 tablespoons chopped fresh parsley

black olives, lemon slices and parsley, to
garnish

DRESSING:

75 ml (2½ fl oz/⅓ cup) virgin olive oil

1 tablespoon red wine vinegar

Put beans and flageolets into a bowl with onion and season with salt and pepper. Add tuna fish, breaking it into large flakes. Stir in parsley.

To make the dressing, put ingredients in a bowl or screw-top jar, mix well, then add to salad. Toss gently, then transfer to dish. Serve garnished with black olives, lemon slices and parsley.

*Serves 4 as a main course and
6 as a starter.*

— MEDITERRANEAN LENTILS —

250 g (8 oz/1¼ cups) brown or green lentils

250 g (8 oz) tomatoes, skinned, seeded and diced

3 sticks celery, sliced

125 g (4 oz) button mushrooms, sliced

celery leaves and lemon slices, to garnish

SPICY LEMON DRESSING:

75 ml (2½ fl oz/⅓ cup) virgin olive oil

1 tablespoon lemon juice

1 clove garlic, crushed

1 tablespoon chopped fresh parsley

½ teaspoon ground cumin

salt and pepper

Put the lentils in a sieve and rinse thoroughly, then tip into a saucepan and cover with water. Bring to the boil, then simmer for 30 minutes until tender. Drain and put into a bowl with the tomatoes, celery and mushrooms.

To make the dressing. Put all the ingredients in a bowl or screw-top jar and mix well. Pour over the salad and stir. Serve garnished with celery leaves and lemon slices.

Serves 6 as a side salad.

BULGAR MEDLEY

2 tablespoons sunflower oil
2 shallots, chopped
1 clove garlic, crushed
250 g (8 oz) bulgar wheat
500 ml (16 fl oz/2 cups) hot vegetable stock
2 carrots, diced
3 sticks celery, sliced
3 leeks, sliced
2 courgettes (zucchini), diced
fresh mint leaves, to garnish
GARLIC TOMATO DRESSING:
250 g (8 oz) tomatoes, skinned, seeded and finely chopped
3 tablespoons virgin olive oil
1 tablespoon wine vinegar
1 teaspoon tomato purée (paste)
1 clove garlic, crushed
½ teaspoon paprika
pinch sugar
salt and pepper

Heat oil in a saucepan, add shallots and garlic and cook for 2-3 minutes. Add bulgar wheat and stir for 1 minute over a medium heat. Gradually pour in hot stock and simmer for 5 minutes. Add carrots, celery and leeks and cook for 5 minutes. Stir in courgettes and cook for a further 2 minutes. Set aside.

To make the dressing, mix all the ingredients together in a bowl, then stir into bulgar salad. Leave to cool, then check the seasoning.

Serve garnished with fresh mint leaves.

Serves 6-8 as a side salad.

Variation: Other lightly cooked vegetables can be substituted for the ones used here.

SPROUTED BEAN SALAD

60 g (2 oz) aduki beans
60 g (2 oz/⅓ cup) mung beans
60 g (2 oz/⅓ cup) green lentils
1 purple onion
HONEY MUSTARD DRESSING:
60 ml (2 fl oz/¼ cup) Mayonnaise, see page 12
2 tablespoons sunflower oil
1 tablespoon clear honey
1 tablespoon prepared mild mustard
1 tablespoon lemon juice
salt and pepper

Start this salad 4-6 days before you want to serve it. Put each of the beans in a bowl, cover with water and leave to soak overnight. Drain and put each variety into a wide-neck jar. Cover with muslin, secure with elastic bands and place all the jars in a warm, dark place such as an airing cupboard.

Twice a day, fill the jars with water, drain through the muslin to rinse the beans. The beans will have sprouted in 4-6 days. Remove the sprouted beans from the jars and rinse again.

To make the dressing, beat all the ingredients together in a bowl until the honey is evenly blended. Slice the onion and mix with the sprouted beans. Place in a serving dish and add the dressing. Toss the salad until all the sprouts are coated and serve immediately.

Serves 6 as a side salad.

Note: The sprouted beans can be stored in the refrigerator for up to 4 days.

BUTTER BEAN SALAD

250 g (8 oz) dried butter beans, soaked overnight

salt

185 g (6 oz) streaky bacon, rinds removed

snipped chives, to garnish

TOMATO DRESSING:

185 g (6 oz) tomatoes, skinned, seeded and chopped

1 teaspoon tomato purée (paste)

3 tablespoons extra virgin olive oil

2 teaspoons lemon juice

salt and pepper

Rinse butter beans, put into a saucepan, cover with water and simmer for about 1 hour until tender. Add salt during last 5 minutes of cooking.

Meanwhile, cook bacon in a frying pan until crisp. Remove from the pan and drain on absorbent kitchen paper, then crumble into small pieces.

To make the dressing, put all the ingredients into a blender and work until tomatoes are pulpy. Drain beans, put into a serving dish and pour over the dressing. Mix in bacon. Leave to cool. Serve garnished with snipped chives.

Serves 4-6 as a side salad.

JADE SALAD

250 g (8 oz/1 ⅓ cups) long grain rice

250 g (8 oz) frozen chopped spinach, thawed

1 bunch spring onions, trimmed

2 tablespoons chopped fresh parsley

salt and pepper

½ quantity Vinaigrette Dressing, see page 10

Cook the rice in a saucepan of boiling salted water for 10-12 minutes until tender. Drain, rinse with fresh boiling water, then drain.

Squeeze as much water from spinach as possible, then put into a salad bowl. Reserve 2 spring onions to cut into tassels, then finely chop the rest. Add to the bowl with the spinach, parsley and seasoning. Add rice and, while still warm, stir in dressing and mix. Allow salad to cool completely, then chill before serving. Serve garnished with spring onion tassels.

Serves 6.

CURRIED RICE SALAD

90 g (3 oz) semi-dried apricots, chopped
250 g (8 oz/1⅓ cups) long grain brown rice
3 tablespoons sunflower oil
60 g (2 oz/⅓ cup) cashew nuts
1 onion, chopped
1 teaspoon cumin seeds
3 teaspoons curry powder
90 ml (3 fl oz/⅓ cup) orange juice
60 g (2 oz/⅓ cup) raisins
salt and pepper
coriander sprigs, to garnish

Put chopped apricots in a bowl, pour over sufficient boiling water to cover and leave to soak for 45 minutes.

Meanwhile, cook rice in boiling salted water for 40 minutes until tender.

Heat the oil in a frying pan, add cashew nuts and fry until golden.

Remove with a slotted spoon and drain on absorbent kitchen paper. Add onion to pan and cook over a medium heat for 3-4 minutes. Stir in cumin seeds and curry powder and cook for 2 minutes. Pour in orange juice and simmer for 1 minute. Remove from heat.

Drain rice, rinse under cold running water, then drain again. Put into a large bowl, add the warm curry sauce and mix well.

Drain apricots and stir into rice with nuts and raisins. Season with salt and pepper. Allow the salad to stand for at least 2 hours before serving to allow flavours to mingle. Serve garnished with sprigs of fresh coriander.

Serves 6 as a side salad.

MEXICAN BEAN SALAD

440 g (14 oz) can red kidney beans, drained

185 g (6 oz) frozen sweetcorn, cooked

1 green pepper (capsicum), seeded and chopped

½ bunch spring onions, chopped

2 tablespoons chopped fresh coriander

½ iceberg lettuce, shredded, if desired

lime slices and parsley sprigs, to garnish

LIME DRESSING:

60 ml (2 fl oz/¼ cup) virgin olive oil

juice of ½ lime

1 clove garlic, crushed

salt and pepper

Put the kidney beans, sweetcorn, green pepper (capsicum), spring onions and coriander into a bowl.

To make the dressing, put all the ingredients into a bowl or screw-top jar and mix well. Pour over the salad and toss together.

Line a serving dish with the shredded iceberg lettuce, if desired, and spoon the bean mixture on top. Serve the salad garnished with lime slices and sprigs of parsley.

Serves 4-6 as a side salad.

TABBOULEH

185 g (6 oz) bulgar wheat

60 ml (2 fl oz/¼ cup) lemon juice

60 ml (2 fl oz/¼ cup) virgin olive oil

1 tablespoon finely chopped Spanish onion

6 spring onions, finely chopped

90 g (3 oz) bunch flat leaf parsley, chopped

30 g (1 oz) fresh mint, chopped

salt and pepper

1 cos lettuce

cherry tomatoes and parsley sprigs, to garnish

Put bulgar into a bowl, cover with warm water and leave to soak for 30 minutes. Squeeze out excess water and put bulgar into a bowl. Add lemon juice, oil, onion, spring onions, parsley and mint and season to taste with salt and pepper. Mix together, then chill for a least 1 hour.

To serve, arrange cos lettuce leaves around the edge of a platter, spoon salad in the centre and garnish with cherry tomatoes and sprigs of parsley.

Serves 6.

— SPICED CHICK-PEA SALAD —

375 g (12 oz/2 cups) dried chick-peas,
soaked overnight

2 tablespoons chopped fresh coriander and
coriander sprigs, to garnish

CORIANDER DRESSING:

3 tablespoons olive oil

1 small onion, chopped

1 green chilli, seeded and finely chopped

1 clove garlic, finely chopped

2 teaspoons ground coriander

1 teaspoon ground cumin

1 teaspoon turmeric

salt and pepper

2 tablespoons natural yogurt

Drain chick-peas from soaking water and put into a saucepan with fresh water. Bring to the boil, and simmer for 1 hour or until tender.

Meanwhile, make the dressing. Heat oil in a small frying pan, add onion, chilli and garlic and cook for 2-3 minutes. Stir in spices and cook for 1 minute. Season to taste with salt and pepper. Turn into a large bowl and stir in the yogurt.

Drain chick-peas, cool briefly then remove skins while still warm. Add to spice mixture and mix well. Leave to marinate for at least 2 hours. Serve garnished with the coriander.

Serves 6 as a side salad.

– JAPANESE VINEGARED SALAD –

125 g (4 oz) mange tout (snow peas), trimmed
185 g (6 oz/1 cup) long grain rice
JAPANESE DRESSING:
2 tablespoons rice vinegar
1 tablespoon light sesame oil
1 teaspoon dark sesame oil
4 teaspoons tamari (Japanese soy sauce)
4 spring onions, chopped

Blanch the mange tout (snow peas) in a saucepan of boiling water for 30 seconds, drain, rinse under cold water, then dry on absorbent kitchen paper. Arrange around edge of serving dish.

Cook rice in boiling salted water for 10-12 minutes until tender. Drain, rinse with cold water, then drain again. Put rice into a bowl. To make the dressing, mix ingredients together in a bowl or screw-top jar. Stir into rice. Spoon rice into serving dish and serve.

Serves 4-6.

Variation: The dressed rice can be wrapped in small blanched spinach or vine leaves. Cut the parcels in half, then stand them on end to resemble Japanese sushi.

HUMMUS SALAD

470 g (15 oz) can chick-peas, drained
60 ml (2 fl oz/¼ cup) virgin olive oil
3 tablespoons tahini (sesame seed paste)
2 cloves garlic
juice of 1 lemon
salt and pepper
1 teaspoon paprika
olives and coriander leaves, to garnish
TO SERVE:
carrot sticks or baby carrots
celery sticks
radishes

Put chick-peas in a blender or food processor with 3 tablespoons of oil, tahini, garlic and lemon juice. Work until smooth, then season.

Spoon into a serving bowl or 4 individual dishes. Drizzle remaining oil over and dust with paprika.

Garnish and serve with the raw fresh vegetables.

Serves 4 as a starter or light meal.

THREE BEAN SALAD

125 g (4 oz) dried red kidney beans, soaked overnight

salt and pepper

185 g (6 oz) thin green beans, trimmed and cut into 4 cm (1½ in) lengths

250 g (8 oz) shelled broad beans

shallot rings, to garnish

SHALLOT DRESSING:

60 ml (2 fl oz/¼ cup) virgin olive oil

1 tablespoon red wine vinegar

1 shallot, finely chopped

Put red kidney beans into a saucepan with water to cover and boil for 1½ hours until tender, adding salt 5 minutes before the end of the cooking time. Drain, put into a bowl, and leave to cool.

Cook green beans and broad beans in boiling salted water for about 5 minutes until just tender. Drain, skin broad beans, and add both beans to the kidney beans.

To make the dressing, mix ingredients together in a bowl or screw-top jar, seasoning to taste with salt and pepper. Pour over the salad and toss. Transfer to a serving dish, cover and refrigerate until required. Serve garnished with shallot rings.

Serves 4-6.

— THOUSAND ISLAND SALAD —

750 g (1½ lb) firm white fish, such as bass, cod, halibut, swordfish, monkfish
juice of 1 lemon
salt and pepper
2 kiwi fruit
2 tamarillos
1 small mango
paprika and parsley sprigs, to garnish
THOUSAND ISLAND DRESSING:
1 quantity Mayonnaise, see page 12
1 teaspoon tomato purée (paste)
3 teaspoons lemon juice
6 stuffed olives, chopped
2 spring onions, finely chopped
1 tablespoon chopped fresh parsley
1 hard-boiled egg, chopped
½ teaspoon paprika
½ teaspoon sugar

Preheat oven to 190C (375F/Gas 5). Skin the fish and put into an ovenproof dish, sprinkle over lemon juice and season with salt and pepper. Cook in the oven for 15-20 minutes. Allow to cool, then cut into cubes. Spoon over a little of the cooking juices to keep the fish moist.

Meanwhile, make the dressing by mixing all the ingredients together in a bowl.

Prepare the fruit. Peel the kiwi fruit and tamarillos, then slice. Peel the mango and cut into sticks.

Divide the fish between 4 plates, arrange the tropical fruits around the fish, then either spoon over the dressing or serve it on one side. Garnish fish with a little paprika and sprigs of parsley.

Serves 4 as a main course.

— GINGER PORK & LYCHEES —

2 tablespoons light sesame oil
500 g (1 lb) pork fillet, cut into strips
1 clove garlic, crushed
1 tablespoon chopped fresh ginger
90 g (3 oz) mange tout (snow peas), cut into thin strips
470 g (15 oz) can lychees, drained
½ head Chinese leaves
chilli flowers, to garnish
SWEET AND SOUR DRESSING:
2 tablespoons light sesame oil
4 teaspoons rice vinegar
2 teaspoons dark soy sauce
1 teaspoon honey
1 teaspoon tomato purée (paste)

Heat oil in a large frying pan or wok, add pork, garlic and ginger and cook until pork is lightly browned. Add mange tout (snow peas) and cook for 30 seconds. Remove from heat, transfer with a slotted spoon, and add lychees.

To make the dressing, mix ingredients together in a bowl. Pour over salad, then leave to cool.

Shred Chinese leaves, arrange on serving platter or dishes. Spoon salad on top, garnish and serve.

Serves 4 as a main course.

— CHICKEN & GRAPE SALAD —

500 g (1 lb) cooked cold chicken, cut into small dice

3 sticks celery, chopped

125 g (4 oz) black grapes

125 g (4 oz) green grapes

½ lettuce, finely shredded, if desired

nasturtium flowers and tarragon sprigs, to garnish

TARRAGON CREAM DRESSING:

3 tablespoons virgin olive oil

1 tablespoon tarragon vinegar

3 tablespoons thick sour cream

salt and pepper

Put chicken and celery in a bowl. Halve grapes, remove pips and add to the bowl.

To make the dressing, mix all the ingredients together in a bowl or screw-top jar. Pour over salad and toss together. Divide lettuce, if using, between 4 plates and spoon chicken salad on top. Serve garnished with nasturtium flowers and tarragon.

Serves 4 as a main course.

─── ROLLMOP & APPLE SALAD ───

8 rollmop herrings
2 green eating apples
2 tablespoons lemon juice
1 bulb fennel, finely sliced
hard-boiled egg slices and dill sprigs, to garnish
SOUR CREAM DILL DRESSING:
155 ml (5 fl oz/²⁄₃ cup) carton thick sour cream
2 tablespoons natural yogurt
2 teaspoons creamed horseradish sauce
1 tablespoon chopped fresh dill
salt and pepper

Cut rollmops into bite-sized pieces and put into a bowl. Core and chop apples, put into a second bowl with lemon juice; toss to prevent discolouration. Remove apple and add to the herrings with the fennel.

To make the dressing, mix ingredients together in a bowl, then stir into the salad. Transfer to a serving dish and serve garnished with slices of hard-boiled egg and sprigs of dill.

Serves 4 as a main course.

— CHEESE & FRUIT PLATTER —

2 green eating apples
juice of ½ lemon
125 g (4 oz) smoked cheese, cubed
250 g (8 oz) brie, or 1 whole camembert, sliced
4 sticks celery, sliced
185 g (6 oz) grapes
celery leaves or mustard and cress, to garnish
LEMON MAYONNAISE:
½ quantity Mayonnaise, see page 12
½ teaspoon finely grated lemon peel
2 teaspoons lemon juice

Quarter and core the apples, then slice and place in a bowl with the lemon juice. Stir to coat. Arrange cubed and sliced the cheese and the apple slices on 4 plates.

Make an attractive pattern with the celery and grapes. Garnish with celery leaves or mustard and cress. To make the mayonnaise, mix all the ingredients together in a bowl. Serve the mayonnaise separately.

Serves 4.

— TURKEY & CRANBERRY SALAD —

500 g (1 lb) turkey escalopes
2 tablespoons virgin olive oil
1 small onion, chopped
125 g (4 oz) fresh or frozen cranberries
grated peel of ½ orange
orange slices and watercress sprigs, to garnish
MARINADE:
juice of 1 lime
125 ml (4 fl oz/½ cup) dry vermouth
2 teaspoons clear honey
½ teaspoon dry oregano
salt and pepper

Cut the turkey escalopes into thin strips. Mix marinade ingredients together in a bowl. Add turkey strips and marinate for 2 hours.

Remove turkey from marinade with a slotted spoon; reserve marinade. Heat oil in a frying pan, add turkey and onion and sauté for 5 minutes. Pour reserved marinade into the pan with the cranberries and orange peel and cook gently until the cranberries begin to split. Transfer the mixture to a dish to cool.

Stir the salad and spoon into a serving dish. Serve garnished with orange slices and sprigs of watercress.

Serves 3-4 as a main course.

— NECTARINES & PROSCIUTTO —

mixed salad leaves
2 nectarines or peaches
125 g (4 oz) prosciutto (cured ham)
fresh raspberries, to garnish, if desired
RASPBERRY VINAIGRETTE:
3 tablespoons virgin olive oil
5 teaspoons sunflower oil
3 teaspoons raspberry vinegar

Divide salad leaves between 4 plates.

Slice nectarines, halve slices of proscuitto (cured ham) and wrap around the fruit. Arrange on the salad leaves.

To make the dressing, mix ingredients together in a bowl or screw-top jar. Drizzle over the salad, then serve garnished with fresh raspberries, if desired.

Serves 4 as a starter.

— AVOCADO & STRAWBERRIES —

2 avocados
250 g (8 oz) strawberries, hulled
mint or strawberry leaves, to garnish
HONEY LEMON DRESSING:
2 tablespoons sunflower oil
2 teaspoons lemon juice
¼ teaspoon paprika
salt and pepper

To make the dressing, put all the ingredients in a bowl or screw-top jar and mix well. Set aside

Cut avocados in half, remove stones and peel. Dice the flesh and put into a bowl. If strawberries are large, slice or halve them, then add to avocado. Pour over dressing and toss together.

Divide between 4 dishes and serve garnished with leaves.

Serves 4 as a starter.

— PRAWNS WITH GRAPEFRUIT —

60 g (2 oz) young spinach leaves
1 bunch watercress, trimmed
2 ruby red grapefruit
185 g (6 oz) peeled cooked prawns
2 teaspoons chopped fresh chervil, to garnish
GRAPEFRUIT YOGURT DRESSING:
2 tablespoons Greek strained yogurt
2 tablespoons virgin olive oil
1 teaspoon clear honey
salt and pepper

Wash spinach, dry and tear leaves into smaller pieces. Mix with watercress, then divide between 4 individual serving dishes.

Cut peel and pith from grapefruit. Holding each one over a bowl to catch juice, remove segments. Arrange the segments over the salad, then scatter the prawns over the top.

To make the dressing, mix all the ingredients together in a bowl with 2 tablespoons of the reserved grapefruit juice, then spoon over the salads. Serve garnished with chervil.

Serves 4 as a starter.

— MELON & TOMATO SALAD —

1 small honeydew melon or 2 galia, cantaloupe or rock melons	
375 g (12 oz) tomatoes, skinned	
mint sprigs, to garnish	
MINT DRESSING:	
2 tablespoons sunflower oil	
2 teaspoons sherry vinegar	
1 tablespoon chopped fresh mint	
pepper	

Cut melon or melons in half, remove seeds, then cut the flesh into cubes (or balls using a melon scoop) and place in a bowl.

Quarter the tomatoes, remove seeds and cut each wedge across into 4 pieces. Add to the melon.

To make the dressing, mix all the ingredients together in a bowl or screw-top jar. Pour over the salad and stir gently. Cover well and chill for flavours to mingle.

Remove from refrigerator 30 minutes before serving. Spoon into 4 dishes or, if using the smaller variety of melons, spoon salad into the shells. Serve garnished with sprigs of mint.

Serves 4 as a starter.

WALDORF SALAD

3 red eating apples
3 tablespoons lemon juice
5 sticks celery
60 g (2 oz/⅓ cup) walnuts, roughly chopped
½ teaspoon caraway seeds
125 ml (4 fl oz/½ cup) Mayonnaise, see page 12
walnut halves and celery leaves, to garnish

Cut apples into quarters and remove cores; dice them and put into a bowl with lemon juice.

Thinly slice celery, add to the apple with the walnuts and caraway seeds. Mix together, then stir in the mayonnaise.

Spoon the apple and celery into a bowl and serve garnished with walnut halves and celery leaves.

Serves 6 as a side salad.

— CHICORY & ORANGE SALAD —

60 g (2 oz/⅓ cup) hazelnuts
4 heads chicory, chopped
3 oranges
1 tablespoon chopped fresh parsley
HAZELNUT DRESSING:
3 tablespoons hazelnut oil
3 tablespoons orange juice
pinch mixed spice
salt and pepper

Place hazelnuts on baking sheet and brown under a hot grill until the skins begin to crack. Allow to cool a little, then rub off the skins. Roughly chop the nuts. Put chicory in a large bowl.

Cut peel and pith from oranges. Holding each one over a bowl to catch juice, cut into segments. Cut the segments in half and add to the chicory.

To make the dressing, add all the ingredients to the juice in a bowl, mix well, then pour over the salad. Toss gently, then transfer to a serving dish. Scatter over the hazelnuts and serve garnished with chopped parsley.

Serves 4-6 as a side salad.

— AVOCADO & CITRUS SALAD —

½ curly endive, torn into pieces
2 oranges
1 grapefruit
1 ripe avocado
CITRUS DRESSING:
3 teaspoons sunflower oil
peel and juice of ½ lime
1 tablespoon chopped fresh mint
salt and pepper

Put endive into a salad bowl. Cut peel and pith from oranges and grapefruit. Holding each one over a bowl to catch juice, remove segments and halve. Arrange on top of endive.

Halve avocado, remove stone, slice or dice flesh, then add to salad.

To make the dressing, mix all the ingredients in a bowl or screw-top jar with 2 tablespoons of juice. Spoon over salad, and serve.

Serves 4 as a side salad.

— PERSIAN CARROT SALAD —

500 g (1 lb) carrots, grated
2 large oranges
90 g (3 oz/¹⁄₂ cup) raisins
60 g (2 oz/¹⁄₃ cup) blanched almonds, lightly toasted
lime slices, to garnish
SPICY DRESSING:
2 tablespoons virgin olive oil
2 tablespoons lime juice
1 teaspoon ground cumin
¹⁄₂ teaspoon ground cinnamon
¹⁄₂ teaspoon caster sugar

Put carrots into a bowl. Cut peel and pith from oranges. Remove segments and chop. Add to carrots with raisins and almonds.

To make the dressing, mix all the ingredients together in a bowl or screw-top jar. Add to salad. Toss together, then refrigerate for 1 hour. Serve garnished with lime slices.

Serves 6 as a side salad.

FRUITY COLESLAW

375 g (12 oz) white or light green cabbage, finely shredded
440 g (14 oz) can pineapple slices or 375 g (12 oz) fresh pineapple, chopped
1½ eating apples
2 teaspoons lemon juice
90 g (3 oz/½ cup) raisins
60 g (2 oz/⅓ cup) salted peanuts
½ apple, sliced, or pineapple leaves to garnish
DRESSING:
1 quantity Mayonnaise, see page 12
1 teaspoon clear honey
3 tablespoons pineapple or apple juice
salt and pepper

Put cabbage into a large bowl. If using canned pineapple, drain well, reserving the juice, and chop the fruit. Add pineapple to cabbage.

Core and chop apples, toss in lemon juice and add to salad with raisins and peanuts.

To make the dressing, mix all the ingredients in a bowl, using reserved pineapple juice or apple juice, then pour over the salad. Mix well, then turn into a serving dish. Garnish and serve at once.

Serves 6-8 as a side salad.

— APPLE & CELERIAC SALAD —

1 celeriac
3 eating apples
2 tablespoons lemon juice
POPPY SEED DRESSING:
2 tablespoons poppy seeds
60 g (2 oz / ¼ cup) thick natural yogurt
3 tablespoons apple juice
salt and pepper

Peel celeriac; cut into 1 cm (½ in) thick slices. Put into a saucepan of boiling water and simmer for 7-8 minutes until just tender. Drain and leave to cool.

Cut apples into quarters; remove cores. Slice 4 quarters; dice remainder. Put all the apple into a bowl with lemon juice and toss together.

Remove apple slices, put to one side for garnishing. Dice the celeriac and mix with the diced apples.

To make the dressing, mix all the ingredients together in a screw-top jar, then pour over the salad and toss together. Transfer to a serving dish and serve garnished with apple slices.

Serves 6 as a side salad.

— CLASSIC TOMATO SALAD —

500 g (1 lb) firm tomatoes
1 teaspoon sugar
salt and pepper
90 ml (3 fl oz / ⅓ cup) virgin olive oil
2 tablespoons white wine vinegar
1 tablespoon snipped chives
chopped mixed fresh herbs, to garnish

Slice tomatoes thinly and arrange on a serving plate. Sprinkle with sugar and season with salt and pepper. Mix oil and vinegar together in a bowl or screw-top jar, then spoon over the salad.

Scatter over chives, then cover salad and refrigerate for a least 1 hour before serving. Garnish with mixed herbs.

Serves 4-6.

Variation: Sprinkle tomatoes with finely chopped spring onion or shredded basil instead of chives.

— GERMAN POTATO SALAD —

1 kg (2 lb) potatoes, scrubbed
6 spring onions, finely chopped
salt and pepper
3 tablespoons Mayonnaise, see page 12
3 tablespoons natural yogurt
snipped chives, to garnish

Cook unpeeled potatoes in a saucepan of boiling salted water for about 15 minutes until tender.

Drain, then cool a little before removing skins. Cool completely. Dice potatoes and put into a bowl with spring onions, then season with salt and pepper.

Mix mayonnaise and yogurt together in a bowl, then fold into the salad. Spoon into serving dish and serve garnished with chives.

Serves 6.

Note: The potato skins can be left on if preferred.

— BEETROOT & ONION SALAD —

500 g (1 lb) cooked beetroot
2 shallots, finely chopped
60 ml (2 fl oz/¼ cup) Vinaigrette Dressing, see page 10
1 lettuce, separated into leaves
½ small onion, cut into thin rings
chopped fresh parsley, to garnish

Cut beetroot into matchsticks. Put into a bowl and mix with shallots and dressing. Leave to marinate for 2 hours.

Line a serving bowl with lettuce leaves, spoon beetroot on top and scatter over onion rings. Serve garnished with chopped parsley.

Serves 4-6.

COLESLAW

500 g (1 lb) white cabbage, shredded
2 carrots, coarsely grated
5 sticks celery, sliced
2 tablespoons chopped fresh parsley
celery leaves, to garnish
BOILED DRESSING:
2 tablespoons sunflower oil
3 teaspoons flour
2 teaspoons vinegar
1 teaspoon dry mustard
1 egg, beaten
salt and pepper
pinch cayenne pepper

Put cabbage, carrots, celery and parsley into a bowl and mix well.

To make the dressing, blend oil and flour in a saucepan, add 125 ml (4 fl oz/½ cup) water, the vinegar, mustard, egg and seasonings. Cook over a very low heat until thickened, stirring all the time. Cool slightly, then pour over the salad and mix well. Cool before serving garnished with celery leaves.

Serves 6-8.

GREEK SALAD

½ cos lettuce, chopped
a few young spinach leaves, shredded
3 tomatoes, cut into wedges
½ cucumber, halved lengthwise and sliced
½ Spanish onion, cut into rings
1 green pepper (capsicum), seeded and sliced
185 g (6 oz) feta cheese, cubed
12 black olives
1 teaspoon chopped fresh oregano
LEMON DRESSING:
60 ml (2 fl oz/¼ cup) extra virgin olive oil
1 tablespoon lemon juice
salt and pepper

Put lettuce, spinach, tomatoes, cucumber, onion and pepper (capsicum) into a bowl. Top with cheese and olives; sprinkle with oregano.

Mix dressing ingredients. Spoon over the salad and serve.

Serves 4.

CAULIFLOWER SALAD

1 cauliflower
1 bunch radishes, trimmed and sliced
toasted sesame seeds
radishes, to garnish
TAHINI DRESSING:
155 ml (5 fl oz/²⁄₃ cup) natural yogurt
4 teaspoons tahini (sesame seed paste)
1 teaspoon clear honey

Break cauliflower into small flowerets, blanch in a saucepan of boiling water for 2 minutes, drain and cool. Put into a bowl with radishes.

To make the dressing, mix all the ingredients together in a bowl. Pour onto salad and mix well. Spoon into a serving dish and sprinkle with sesame seeds. Serve garnished with radishes.

Serves 6.

— WHOLEWHEAT PASTA SALAD —

125 g (4 oz) wholewheat pasta shapes	
185 g (6 oz) shelled broad beans	
250 g (8 oz) broccoli flowerets	
90 g (3 oz) mange tout (snow peas), trimmed	
3 tomatoes, diced	
½ recipe Garlic Vinaigrette, see page 11	
herbs sprigs, to garnish	

Cook pasta in a saucepan of boiling salted water for 12-15 minutes until just tender. Drain, rinse with cold water, and drain again. Put into a bowl.

Cook broad beans in a saucepan of boiling salted water for 15 minutes until tender; drain. Cool slightly, then remove skins while still warm.

Steam broccoli and mange tout (snow peas) in a colander over a saucepan of boiling water for 3 minutes. Leave vegetables to cool, then add to the pasta with the tomatoes. Spoon over the vinaigrette and toss well. Transfer salad to a serving dish and serve garnished with sprigs of herbs.

Serves 4-6.

CHINATOWN SALAD

125 g (4 oz) baby sweetcorn
250 g (8 oz) can water chestnuts, drained
½ red pepper (capsicum), seeded and sliced
5 cm (2 in) piece cucumber
185 g (6 oz) beansprouts, trimmed
1 cm (½ in) piece fresh ginger, finely shredded
1 quantity Sesame Dressing, see page 15
coriander leaves, to garnish

Cook sweetcorn in a saucepan of boiling water for 5 minutes, drain and cool. Slice water chestnuts and put into a bowl with sweetcorn and pepper (capsicum).

Slice cucumber lengthwise, then diagonally into strips and add to the salad with beansprouts and ginger; mix together.

Pour over the dressing and toss gently. Spoon into a serving dish and serve garnished with coriander.

Serves 6.

FRENCH POTATO SALAD

750 g (1½ lb) new potatoes, scrubbed
1 tablespoon virgin olive oil
2 tablespoons chopped mixed herbs and herb sprigs
HERB VINAIGRETTE:
3 tablespoons virgin olive oil
1 tablespoon white wine vinegar
salt and pepper

Boil unpeeled potatoes in a saucepan of salted water for about 15 minutes until tender. Drain. If they are small leave whole, otherwise cool a little, then cut into slices, halves or quarters. Put into a bowl and, while still warm, pour over 1 tablespoon oil. Leave to cool.

To make the dressing, mix together oil and vinegar in a bowl or screw-top jar. Season with salt and pepper, then stir into potatoes. Just before serving, sprinkle with chopped herbs and gently fold in. Garnish with sprigs of herbs.

Serves 4-6.

WINTER RED SALAD

1 oakleaf lettuce or other red lettuce
1 head radicchio
1 purple onion, sliced
125 g (4 oz) red cabbage, shredded
185 g (6 oz) cooked beetroot, diced
pomegranate seeds, to garnish
WALNUT VINAIGRETTE:
2 tablespoons walnut oil
1 tablespoon virgin olive oil
1 tablespoon red wine vinegar
½ teaspoon Dijon mustard
pinch sugar
salt and pepper

Arrange salad leaves in a bowl. Add the onion, cabbage and beetroot.

To make the dressing, mix all the ingredients together in a bowl or screw-top jar, add to salad and toss gently. Serve garnished with pomegranate seeds.

Serves 4-6.

COURGETTE SALAD

500 g (1 lb) courgettes (zucchini), coarsely grated
salt
fresh herbs or baby courgettes (zucchini) and flowers, to garnish
HERB YOGURT MAYONNAISE:
2 tablespoons Mayonnaise, see page 12
2 teaspoons chopped fresh parsley
2 teaspoons chopped fresh tarragon
2 teaspoons chopped fresh chervil
2 teaspoons chopped fresh chives
60 ml (2 fl oz/¼ cup) natural yogurt
pepper

Place courgettes (zucchini) on 3 layers of absorbent kitchen paper, sprinkle with salt and leave for 1 hour.

To make the dressing, mix all the ingredients together in a large bowl. Add courgettes (zucchini) to dressing and stir together. Spoon into a serving dish and serve garnished with fresh herbs or baby courgettes (zucchini) and flowers.

Serves 6.

— TRICOLOUR PASTA SALAD —

250 g (8 oz) tricoloured pasta twists
salt
1 tablespoon virgin olive oil
125 g (4 oz) open-caped mushrooms, sliced (use wild mushrooms if available)
90 g (3 oz) green olives, stoned and chopped
60 g (2 oz) can anchovies, drained and cut into thin strips
1 tablespoon chopped fresh oregano
oregano sprigs, to garnish
DRESSING:
2 tablespoons virgin olive oil
1 tablespoon balsamico vinegar
pepper

Cook pasta in boiling salted water for 5-6 minutes until just tender, then drain and rinse under cold water and drain again.

Heat the oil in a frying pan and cook the mushrooms for 2-3 minutes. Cool, then put into a bowl with the cooked pasta, olives, anchovies and oregano.

To make the dressing, mix together the oil and vinegar and season with pepper. Pour over the salad and toss together. Serve garnished with sprigs of oregano.

Serves 4-6.

SWEET PEPPER SALAD

2 large red peppers (capsicums)
2 large yellow peppers (capsicums)
90 ml (3 fl oz/⅓ cup) extra virgin olive oil
2 cloves garlic
salt and pepper
black olives and fresh parsley, to garnish

Put peppers (capsicums) under a hot grill, turning them until skins are blistered and black all over. Place in a polythene bag and leave to cool for 10-15 minutes. Peel skins off, remove stems and seeds and cut flesh into strips. Arrange in a shallow dish.

Drizzle olive oil over peppers. Peel garlic, cut into slivers and scatter over peppers. Season with salt and pepper, then leave to marinate for 24 hours.

Serve garnished with black olives and parsley.

Serves 4-6.

SUMMER RATATOUILLE

60 ml (2 fl oz / ¼ cup) virgin olive oil
1 bulb fennel, sliced
1 large onion, sliced
1 clove garlic, crushed
1 large beefsteak tomato, peeled and chopped
1 red pepper (capsicum), seeded
1 yellow pepper (capsicum), seeded
1 green pepper (capsicum), seeded
375 g (12 oz) courgettes (zucchini), sliced
1 teaspoon chopped fresh thyme
salt and pepper
shredded basil leaves and fennel fronds, to garnish

Heat oil in a large saucepan, add fennel, onion and garlic, cover and cook gently for 5 minutes. Add tomato; cook for 10 minutes.

Cut peppers (capsicums) into squares, add to pan with courgettes (zucchini) and thyme. Season with salt and pepper and cook for a further 5 minutes. Leave to cool.

Spoon the salad into a serving dish and serve garnished with basil leaves and fennel fronds.

Serves 6.

MOROCCAN SUGARED LETTUCE

1 crisp, curly-leaf lettuce, such as Webb's, escarole or batavia
125 g (4 oz) fresh dates, halved and stoned
3 satsumas or clementines
2 tablespoons caster sugar
3 tablespoons white wine vinegar
pepper

Shred lettuce, then put into salad bowl with the dates.

With a zester, peel shreds of peel from one satsuma or clementine; reserve. Remove peel and pith from fruit, then cut fruit into slices. Break slices into smaller pieces and add to bowl. Sprinkle over sugar and toss salad, then sprinkle over vinegar and toss again. Season with pepper and serve garnished with reserved shreds of peel.

Serves 6.

RADISH SALAD

1 mouli (white radish), weighing about 250 g (8 oz)
salt
1 bunch radishes, trimmed and quartered
1 tablespoon sesame seeds
radish leaves, to garnish
SESAME VINAIGRETTE:
1 tablespoon sunflower oil
1 teaspoon dark sesame oil
2 teaspoons rice vinegar

Grate mouli (white radish) or cut into matchstick strips, place on absorbent kitchen paper and sprinkle with salt. Leave for 30 minutes. Squeeze out any excess moisture, then put mouli (white radish) into a bowl and mix with radishes.

To make the dressing, mix all the ingredients together in a bowl or screw-top jar, then stir into the salad. Spoon salad into a serving dish and serve sprinkled with sesame seeds and garnished with radish leaves.

Serves 6.

— CUCUMBER & DILL SALAD —

1 large cucumber
salt
4 teaspoons lemon juice or white wine vinegar
black pepper, if desired
1 tablespoon chopped fresh dill

Peel cucumber, reserving a few strips of peel. Cut cucumber in half lengthwise and hollow out the seeds with a teaspoon. Slice thinly, then put into a colander, sprinkle with salt and leave to drain for 30 minutes. Rinse with cold water and dry on absorbent paper.

Put cucumber into a bowl and sprinkle with lemon juice or vinegar. Season with pepper, if desired, then stir in dill and serve garnished with strips of cucumber peel.

Serves 4-6.

— ARRANGED GREEN SALAD —

90 g (3 oz) mange tout (snow peas)

250 g (8 oz) fresh asparagus, trimmed

2 avocados

watercress sprigs and alfalfa sprouts, to garnish

LIME AND PISTACHIO DRESSING:

grated peel and juice of ½ lime

1 tablespoon virgin olive oil

1 tablespoon sunflower oil

30 g (1 oz) shelled pistachio nuts

salt and pepper

Blanch mange tout (snow peas) in a saucepan of boiling water for 30 seconds, drain and dry on absorbent kitchen paper. Cook asparagus in boiling water for 7-8 minutes until tender, then drain and cool.

Halve avocados, remove stones and peel. Place, cut side down, on a chopping board and slice crosswise. Gently separate slices and transfer to 4 plates.

Arrange mange tout (snow peas) and asparagus down either side of avocado. To make the dressing, mix all the ingredients together in a bowl or screw-top jar, then spoon over the salad. Garnish with watercress sprigs and alfalfa sprouts.

Serves 4.

WINTER GREEN SALAD

1½ lettuces or mixed salad leaves
250 g (8 oz) broccoli flowerets, trimmed
1 bunch watercress, trimmed
440 g (14 oz) can artichoke hearts, drained
1 bulb fennel, finely sliced
1 green pepper (capsicum), seeded and sliced
GREEN GODDESS DRESSING:
1 quantity Mayonnaise, see page 12
2 anchovy fillets, drained and finely chopped
2 spring onions, finely chopped
2 tablespoons chopped fresh parsley
1 tablespoon tarragon vinegar
1 tablespoon lemon juice
1 clove garlic, crushed
3 tablespoons thick sour cream
salt and pepper

Tear the lettuces into small pieces and put into a serving bowl. Blanch broccoli in a saucepan of boiling water for 2 minutes. Drain, cool, then add to the lettuce with the watercress. Halve the artichoke hearts and add to the salad bowl with the sliced fennel and pepper (capsicum). Toss gently together.

To make the dressing, mix all the ingredients together in a bowl. Spoon a little dressing over the salad, and serve the remainder separately.

Serves 6-8.

Variation: Substitute cauliflower for the broccoli, if preferred.

TOSSED GREEN SALAD

mixture of lettuce to include 2 varieties, such as cos, Webb's, iceberg, Little Gem, endive or batavia
a few young spinach leaves
1 bunch watercress, trimmed
½ cucumber, sliced or diced
1 green pepper (capsicum), seeded and chopped
2 tablespoons chopped mixed fresh herbs, such as parsley, chervil, tarragon, summer savory or chives
DRESSING:
1 clove garlic
salt
1 tablespoon wine vinegar
2 teaspoons lemon juice
¼ teaspoon Dijon mustard
60 ml (2 fl oz/¼ cup) extra virgin olive oil

Tear salad and spinach leaves into smaller pieces. If not using immediately, place in a polythene bag in the refrigerator.

Make the dressing in a wooden salad bowl. Put garlic and a little salt into bowl and crush to a paste with back of a wooden spoon. Add vinegar, lemon juice and mustard, then stir in oil; continue to mix to make an emulsion.

Add all the salad ingredients to the bowl, toss well so that every leaf is coated with dressing. Serve immediately.

Serves 6 as a side salad.

Note: For a less garlicky flavour, rub the inside of the bowl with a cut clove of garlic, then discard.

If you do not have a wooden salad bowl, the dressing can be made separately and poured over just before serving.

CALIFORNIAN SALAD

6 teaspoons powdered gelatine
4 teaspoons sugar
2 lemons
3 tablespoons wine vinegar
few drops yellow food colouring
250 g (8 oz) fresh asparagus, cooked
1 large avocado
2 large carrots, grated
fresh herbs, to garnish

Sprinkle gelatine over 90 ml (3 fl oz/ ⅓ cup) water in a small bowl and leave to soften for 2-3 minutes. Stand bowl in a saucepan of hot water and stir until dissolved. Stir in sugar, then set aside to cool.

Grate the peel from 1 of the lemons and squeeze the juice from both. Reserve 1 tablespoon lemon juice. Put the grated peel and remaining juice into a measuring jug and make up to 940 ml (30 fl oz/ 3¾ cups) with water. Add dissolved gelatine, the vinegar and a few drops of yellow food colouring. Pour a little of the liquid into a 1.8 litre (3 pint/7½ cup) ring mould and refrigerate until the jelly has set.

Cut the tips off the asparagus and arrange on the set jelly. Halve avocado, remove stone, peel, then dice flesh. Place in a bowl and mix with reserved lemon juice. Chop asparagus stalks and add to the avocado with the carrots. Mix well. Stir in remaining liquid, then spoon into the mould. Refrigerate until set.

To serve, turn out the vegetable ring onto a plate and garnish with herbs.

Serves 8.

SUNSHINE SALAD

375 g (12 oz) carrots, cut into matchstick strips

1 yellow pepper (capsicum), seeded and cut into thin strips

1 red pepper (capsicum), seeded and cut into thin strips

125 g (4 oz) frozen sweetcorn, cooked

1 tablespoon sunflower seeds

LEMON MUSTARD VINAIGRETTE:

60 ml (2 fl oz/¼ cup) sunflower oil

5 teaspoons lemon juice

½ teaspoon Dijon mustard

salt and pepper

Arrange strips of carrot round the outer edge of a shallow bowl or plate. Place the pepper (capsicum) strips inside this ring in alternate groups. Spoon the sweetcorn into the centre.

To make the dressing, mix all the ingredients together in a bowl or screw-top jar, then drizzle over the salad. Sprinkle with sunflower seeds just before serving.

Serves 6-8.

INDEX